AN INTRODUCTION TO

Oriental Mythology

CONTRIBUTING EDITOR: CLIO WHITTAKER

AN INTRODUCTION TO

Oriental
Mythology

CONTRIBUTING EDITOR: CLIO WHITTAKER

Grange
BOOKS

A QUINTET BOOK

Published by Grange Books
An imprint of Grange Books plc
The Grange
Grange Yard
London SE1 3AG

This edition published 1995

ISBN 1-85627-820-4

This book was designed and produced by
Quintet Publishing Limited
6 Blundell Street
London N7 9BH

Creative Director: Peter Bridgewater
Art Director: Ian Hunt
Designers: Terry Jeavons/Michael Morey
Illustrations by Lorraine Harrison
Editor: Shaun Barrington
Picture Researcher: Liz Eddison

Typeset in Great Britain by
Central Southern Typesetters, Eastbourne
Manufactured in Hong Kong by
Regent Publishing Services Limited
Printed in Singapore by
Star Standard Industries (Pte) Ltd.

291.13
Ref

Contents

Introduction 6

Chinese Mythology 13

The Giant Pangu 20 · *Nugua Peoples the World 22*
Gonggon's Defeat 24 · *Chang E's Betrayal 27*
The Parted Lovers 32 · *The Great Flood 35*
The Gift of Rice 42 · *Monkey's Immortality 43*

Indian Mythology 51

In the Beginning 54 · *Measuring the Cosmos 58*
Shiva's Blue Throat 64 · *The Death of Sati 65*
The Elephant-headed God 67 · *Kali's Dance of Death 69*
Vishnu the Preserver 72 · *The Young Krishna 72*
The Wrestling Contest 75 · *Hanuman the Monkey God 77*
Spirit of the Buddha 79 · *'Welcome all Three of You' 80*
The Four Virtues 84 · *Princess Badr I Munir 84*

Japanese Mythology 91

Fratricide without Remorse 95 · *Cleansing by Fire 96*
Death of Yamato-Takeru 99 · *Excluded from the Divine 102*
The Birth of Japan 103 · *The Hearth of Yomi 105*
Death Comes to the World 106 · *Part Human, Part Bird 111*
Oni and Kappas 111 · *Buddhist Influence 114*
Soul of the Butterfly 114 · *The Seven Gods 116*

Bibliography 125

Index 126

Acknowledgements 128

Introduction

This book attempts to introduce to the interested reader a taste of the myths and stories of more than one third of the population of the world. The peoples of India, China and Japan are spread over an area of approximately five million square miles, land which covers some of the highest mountain ranges on the globe, barren desert, and tropical forest. The banks of the three great arteries of India and China – the River Ganges, and the Yellow and Yangtse Rivers – are among the most densely populated places to be found on this earth. But also contained within these boundaries are vast tracts of land so inhospitable that they barely accommodate human life – the towering peaks of the Himalayas. As diverse as the geography of the region are the cultural and political experiences of the people: nomadic herdsmen and settled farming com-

ABOVE *The cave complex at Dunhuang in north-western China was begun in* AD 366, *the first to be established in the country; illustrated is the cave of 1,000 Buddhas.*

LEFT *Hindu temple cut from the rock on the sea shore at Mahabalipuram in Madras, India.*

munities, fisher folk who need never set foot on dry land, workers in some of the most modern and innovative industries in the world. Patterns of living that have not changed for centuries exist if not alongside, then not very far from, the most advanced technologies.

The civilizations of the region include some of the most ancient and sophisticated ever to have existed. For more than 3,000 years, the peoples of the East have been trying to give a meaning and purpose to their existence on this earth. This urge to provide an explanation, to account for the otherwise random workings of nature and history, has been felt in all human societies since they came into being. Indeed, it is this need to explain and give significance to life that makes us human. The answers we have pro-

RIGHT *A sandstone bracket in the form of a yakshi, or tree-goddess, from a Jain stupa in Mathura, Uttar Pradesh.*

FAR RIGHT *The Heian shrine was founded in 1895 to celebrate Kyoto's 1,100 years as the capital of Japan.*

BELOW *The horse-shoe shaped ravine at Ajanta, central India, showing the entrances to the 29 Buddhist viharas (monasteries) and chaityas (temples) cut into the rock between the 2nd and 7th centuries AD; inside are some of the earliest surviving examples of Indian painting. Many of the frescoes illustrate the Jataka tales of the Buddha's previous incarnations.*

duced to questions about how the world came to be and our place in it are what we know as myth.

Myths also serve a function of justifying the social order and accounting for the existence of traditional rites and customs. The tales themselves, naturally as rich and diverse as the cultures of which they are a part, have changed as a result of differing social conditions over the centuries. As cultures merge or clash on meeting, so the myths develop and alter.

Mythology is an organic tradition, living off and feeding back into the lives of the people whose existence it enhances.

Given the contrasting and various histories of peoples it is surprising to find that themes occur again and again all over the world. For example, the world-flood, or deluge, which is most familiar to western readers through the story of Noah and the Ark, is to be found in the mythologies of Ireland, Greece, Egypt, Persia, India, Indo-China, Korea, Siberia, Indonesia, the Philippines, Melanesia, Polynesia, Australia, North American Indians, South American Indians, Latin America, and even Africa. One of the main functions of myth is to present a cosmology – that is, to explain how the world came to be. In this book you will find resonances of the Chinese story of Pangu in the tales of Prajapati and Brahma, which originate in India. A symbol of fertility, the egg has been closely connected with creation and birth by many peoples: South Korean myth tells of an egg that contained a baby

ABOVE *Painting of Potala Palace in Lhasa, Tibet; despite the efforts of the Chinese authorities to dissuade the Tibetans – through propaganda and violent repression – from their belief in Buddhism, it remains a potent force.*

who grew up to be leader of the world. But even a concept with such enduring appeal as the egg can be altered and superseded. The ancient account of creation in which the Mediterranean goddess, Eurynome, laid the world-egg from which all nature sprang was replaced by that of Prometheus, who kneaded statuettes of human beings from mud – and the similarities with the Chinese tale of Nugua, which is told here, are striking. The incestuous marriage of Nugua and her brother Fuxi has its counterpart in the Japanese myth of the union of Izanami and Izanagi, almost certainly an example of the borrowing of Chinese ideas that had such important influence on the development of Japanese culture.

The importance that agricultural people attach to the cycle of the seasons and climatic conditions is clearly shown in their mythologies. In China, myths about controlling floods reflect the perennial concern of a farming people whose fortunes depended on channelling the flow of rivers to irrigate their paddy fields; in Japan, an

BELOW *Modern Hindu temple at Matale, near Kandy, Sri Lanka, built in 1973.*
The tower above the main entrance depicts Hindu gods and heroes from the epic poems, the Mahabharata and Ramayana.

ABOVE *Gilded stone carving of the Buddha at Dazu, in central eastern China; 1,500 miles to the east lies Japan, 1,000 miles south is Thailand and a journey 800 miles west, skirting the foothills of the Himalayas, will bring you to Burma and India. Across these vast lands and thousands of miles further, radiates the spirit of the Buddha.*

LEFT *Rahu, one of the nine planets, about to swallow the sun and the moon, thereby causing an eclipse; from Konarak, Orissa, in north-eastern India (13th century).*

9

RIGHT *The Gion
festival, at which
prayers are offered for
the happiness of the
people, is one of the
biggest in Japan, dating
from the 10th century.*

appreciation of the natural world resulting from close observation is incorporated into the Shinto religion. A settled society relying on farming wants its world to follow an ordered and knowable pattern, and a high value is placed on social stability and cohesive family structure; sacrifices and rituals reinforce the sense of community and the greater good. The caste system, which was introduced to Indian caste system, first referred to in the Rig Veda of the Aryan invaders (c 1000 BC), is a system of ensuring her place and function in life. The influence of the caste system in defining individual destinies can still be seen at work today.

The belief in reincarnation, which was already widespread in India by the time of the Buddha, was refined and developed under the influence of Buddhism, which originated in northern India in the 6th century BC. The transmission of Buddhism across the whole continent of Asia – through

BELOW *Buddhist cave
painting at Dunhuang
depicting a group of
mourners at a funeral.
The paintings are
strongly influenced by
Central Asian and
Indian artistic
traditions.*

ABOVE *Contemporary Indian image of Durga, one of the incarnations of Parvati, Shiva's consort.*

its highest expression in Japan.

As in all cultures at all times, the mythologies of Asia have been the inspiration for artistic endeavour. Every area of the arts owes a debt to its mythological heritage: painting, sculpture, architecture, poetry, music – the list is endless. The symbols and stories that have been passed on from generation to generation are a rich and inexhaustible source of wisdom and pleasure. In much of the East, myth is not considered to be a 'dead' subject; it has a vital and necessary part to play in the business of living.

Economists predict that this part of the world will see the most dynamic growth as we enter the last years of the 20th century. It remains to be seen whether the traditions that today exist alongside modern industry and skyscraper cities will survive into the next century. The fact that myths and stories have been an essential part of human life since society came into existence implies that they will.

India and Pakistan to neighbouring Nepal and Tibet, to Sri Lanka and southeast Asia, along the Silk Road to China and from there to Korea and Japan – shows us how a religion, and the myths that are associated with it, develops and grows under differing cultural conditions. The practice of Buddhism, and the art forms it gave rise to, link these countries more than any other factor. The great cave paintings at Dunhuang in the Gansu province of China, show strong Central Asian and Indian influences. As the Chinese civilization is much older than that of Japan, it is not surprising that much borrowing of ideas and techniques occurred. The propagation of Buddhism played an important role in the development of printing in the East, an art form which was to achieve

BELOW *12th–14th century Tibetan figure of Lokapala, Defender of the North, a Lamaistic Buddhist deity. He has nine heads and eighteen arms, and holds a conch, a skull, a toad, pearl, head and vajras. A body is draped over his shoulders, and the flayed skin of a head, hands and feet is draped around his waist. The same image of flayed skin is sometimes seen in Tibetan temple hangings. This one figure includes an amazing richness of symbolic, religious and mythical association.*

Chinese Mythology

The Chinese people have never demanded a clear
separation of the worlds of myth and reality – indeed,
they are so closely bound up that it is hard to say where
one begins and the other ends. Historical figures are
made into gods and myths are recounted as history.
Even in revolutionary China, the same processes could
be seen at work: Chairman Mao, in the heyday of the
Cultural Revolution (1968–78), was often seen as the
all-powerful god responsible for all good things that
happen. When an airline hostess can offer the
explanation that 'there is no need to wear a safety belt,
because Mao, the Great Helmsman, is in charge', the
feeling is that superhuman characters with fantastic
powers, like those that inhabited the ancient texts, are
alive and well in the 20th century.

An apsara, *a heavenly being, in the form of a musician flying on a cloud; this grey*
limestone carving dates from the early 6th century and comes from the Buddhist cave
temples at Longmen, Henan province.

Confusing though the tendency to intertwine fact and fantasy may be for the westerner, it indicates the power and importance of 'mythology' in the Chinese tradition. Chinese people chart their history in an unbroken line back through the dynasties to the world of Nugua and Fuxi, moving seamlessly from a historical to a mythical time-scale. The earliest archaeological evidence supports the existence of the Shang people in the 12th century BC in the basin of the Yellow River, 'the cradle of Chinese civilization', at about the same time as the beginning of Greek culture. As in Greece, by the 4th century BC, China had a society that was highly developed, and many of the distinguishing features of Chinese life then, have been passed down in recognizable form to the 20th century. The achievement of such a striking degree of stability in their social system is one of the Chinese people's most remarkable accomplishments.

The most important means that China used to secure the survival of its social system was its ability to modify and absorb foreign influences. Those who tried to conquer found themselves in confrontation with a society more complex and sophisticated than their own, and even when successful in their military endeavour, usually ended by adopting Chinese practices and political structures. This was the case when the nomadic Manchu tribes conquered China from the north and established the Qing dynasty in the 17th century. But the most significant influence on Chinese development to come from outside its boundaries (that is, until the 20th century and the introduction of

BELOW *Ceremonial axe-head in bronze dating from the Shang dynasty; bronze casting in Shang China was highly developed, in terms of both technique and decoration.*

19th-century Tibetan cloth painting depicting the gruesome fate awaiting sinners after death.

Marxism-Leninism) was not brought by invaders; Buddhism was introduced to China by traders travelling the Silk Road from India and Central Asia during the 1st century BC.

Two religions, or, more accurately, schools of thought, were already well established in China by this time – Confucianism and Taoism. Confucianism is named after its founder Kongfuzi, or Master Kong, who lived between 551–479 BC, during a period known as 'The Warring States'. After a lifetime spent trying in vain to persuade various nobles and rulers of small states to adopt his ideas on ethics and morals, Confucius died without ever seeing his theories put into prac-

tice. His thoughts were collected by his disciples and published post-humously, although it was not until the Han dynasty that Confucianism became the dominant ideology of the Chinese state.

Confucius argued for a highly structured, hierarchical organization of society in which the family was the mainstay of social cohesion. He believed that a state of harmony could be achieved if everyone was aware of their responsibilities and carried out the duties appropriate to their position. Preaching the virtues of filial piety and the veneration of those who had achieved old age ensured that the extended family remained closely

knitted. Although he was non-committal about the existence of supernatural beings, sacrifices were a vital part of Confucius' vision. By carrying out such ceremonies, each was confirmed of his place in the wider scheme of things and reminded of his obligations and duties. For the individual, this took the form of ensuring that one's ancestors were happy and well catered for, both in their dotage and in the afterworld; at state level, the emperor made annual sacrifices to Heaven and Earth. Confucius' concern was a pragmatic one – to ensure the smooth running of a stable, well-ordered state. His philosophy cannot really be said to constitute a 'religion' as it lacks many of the features by which we identify religions, such as a priesthood.

The school of thought known as Taoism came into being about the same time as Confucianism. One of the earliest Taoist texts is a collection of observations, the *Tao Te Ching*, written by the Taoist sage Laozi, around the 6th century BC. At its most philosophical, Taoism argues that there is a natural order in the world that determines the behaviour of all things in existence. Early Taoist thinkers hoped that by studying the world of nature they would discover essential laws. This attention to the spirit of things – particularly naturally occurring phenomena like water or wind – led Taoists into a systematic investigation that became the begin-

ABOVE *17th-century Ming bronze of Laozi, the founder of Taoism. He is shown riding on the water buffalo which carried him away from China to the west.*

RIGHT Summer, *one of a set of paintings by Gong Xian (1652–82), depicting the seasonal changes in the landscape.*

16

ning of science in China. Later on, Taoism operated on a more popular level; the belief that inanimate objects had their own 'spirit' or 'god' gave rise to a system of worship designed to propitiate these powers which was far removed from the early Taoist principles. Taoist priests also practised the art of *fengshui* (wind and water), a method of determining the positioning of buildings so that they did not offend the spirit of the site. Taoism has had great influence on the development of landscape painting in China. Its preoccupations are reflected in the subject matter of the genre – the scholar gazing out from the shelter of a rustic retreat at pine-clad mountains shrouded in mist has been depicted over and over again.

One of the most important contributions that the introduction of Buddhism made to Chinese life was the concept of transmigration of souls. This belief in cyclical life, the view that souls return to the world in a

RIGHT *The Temple of Heaven in Peking, where the emperor conducted the annual sacrifice to Heaven and the prayers for a good harvest.*

17

form determined by their behaviour during their previous incarnation, offered some comfort to those who perhaps felt that their present existence left something to be desired. The mythology of Hell owes most to Buddhism: on arriving in the Underworld, the soul comes before Yen Wang, who examines the register recording all good and evil actions. Those who have done good deeds – for example, filial sons or believers – are able to proceed directly to join the Buddha himself, to go to Mount Kunlun, the home of the immortals, or to be reborn immediately as a human being. Sinners are required to come before one of nine judges who mete out the punishment appropriate to the offences committed. The taking

of life was regarded as the most heinous of Buddhist sins; and it brought about a new respect for living things: vegetarianism became popular as a result of Buddhist influence.

The adage 'Confucian in office, Taoist in retirement and Buddhist as death draws near' sums up the pragmatic Chinese approach to religion. If we aim to rationalize and explain, to codify and authenticate these tales, then we will be exasperated and confounded by the tangled knot that is Chinese mythology. If, on the other hand, we can accept them as meaningful and vivid accounts of a way of experiencing the world, of drawing inspiration and comfort, then we enter a realm that will entrance and delight us.

RIGHT *The massive Leshan Buddha near Chngdu, Sichuan province, is carved out of a cliff overlooking a river.*

RIGHT *The composition of the character* shou, *longevity, is designed to resemble the Taoist diagram of 'inner circulation'; Qing dynasty rubbing.*

THE GIANT PANGU

At the beginning of time there was only dark Chaos in the universe. Into this darkness – which took the form of an egg – Pangu, the first living creature, was born. Pangu slept, nurtured safely inside the egg. After many years, when he had grown into a giant, Pangu awoke and stretched, thereby shattering the egg. The lighter, purer parts of the egg rose up to become the sky; the heavier, impure parts sank down to become the earth. This was the beginning of the forces of *yin* and *yang*.

The female element, *yin*, is associated with cold and darkness, the moon and the earth; the male element, *yang*, with light and warmth, the sun and the heavens. (These ancient Chinese concepts of *yin* and *yang* have become familiar to westerners through the popularization of the *I Ching,* or Book of Changes.)

Pangu feared that heaven and earth might merge together again so he placed himself between them, his head supporting the sky and his feet pressing down on the earth. For the next 18,000 years Pangu grew at a rate of 10 feet a day, increasing the distance between the two by the same amount. Eventually both heaven and earth seemed securely fixed at a gap of 30,000 miles, and Pangu fell into an exhausted sleep from which he never awoke. On his death, the different parts of his body were transformed into the natural elements: his breath became the wind and clouds; his voice turned into thunder and lightning; his left eye became the sun and his right the moon; his four limbs and trunk turned into the cardinal directions and the mountains; his blood formed the rivers and his veins the roads and paths; his flesh became trees and soil; the hair on his head became

the stars in heaven, and the skin and hairs on his body turned into grass and flowers; metals and stones were formed from his teeth and bones, and dew from his sweat. And the various parasites on his body became the different peoples of the human race. Thus was the universe created by the giant Pangu.

There are a number of versions of this myth – although broadly similar they differ in detail about the eventual outcome of the parts of Pangu's body.

Pangu is also sometimes credited with the power to control the weather, the outlook changing according to his temper. Another account of the origin of the human race is given in the following story:

NUGUA PEOPLES THE WORLD

There was once a goddess who was half human and half snake (some say half dragon). She had the ability to change shape and could do so many times a day. One day, as she wandered through this newly-created world, she felt that although there were many wondrous and beautiful things, it was a lonely place. Nugua yearned for the company of beings like herself, with whom she could talk and laugh. She came to a river and sat down on the bank, gazing at her reflection in the

BELOW *Interior of the Hall of Prayer in the Temple of Heaven, Peking.*

22

water. As she mused, she trailed her hand in the water and scooped up some mud from the riverbed. She kneaded the clay into a little figure, only instead of giving it the tail of a snake, like herself, she fashioned legs so it could stand upright. When this little creature was placed on the ground, it at once came to life, prancing around her and laughing with joy. Nugua was very pleased with her handiwork and determined to populate the whole world with these delightful little people. She worked all that day until nightfall, and started again at dawn the next day. But Nugua soon realized that the task she had set herself was immense, and that she would be exhausted before she had made enough people to fill the world. However, by using her supernatural powers, Nugua found she could achieve her wish. She took a length of vine, dipped it in the mud and then whirled it round in the air. The drops of mud that flew off the vine were transformed into little people when they touched the ground. Some say that those who had been formed by Nugua herself became the rich and fortunate people of the earth, and those formed from the drops of mud became the ordinary humble folk. Nugua realized that in order to save the human race from becoming extinct when her original people died, they would need a means of reproducing. So she divided the humans into male and female so they could produce future generations without her assistance.

Another story recounts that long ago there were only two people in the world, Nugua and her brother Fuxi. They wanted to marry and produce children, but were afraid to consummate an incestuous marriage without authority from heaven. One day they

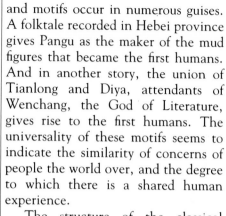

climbed the sacred Mount Kunlun in the west, and each built a bonfire. The smoke from the two fires mingled together and they took this as a sign that they should indeed become husband and wife. Out of modesty, Nugua made herself a fan of straw and with this she covered her face when they were joined together; it is still the custom today for a bride to hold a fan.

These tales contain a number of features that are common to the creation myths of many cultures. The idea of an egg as the beginning of the world occurs in Indian mythology, and the concept of a single progenitor of the human race can be found in cultures as diverse as those of Greece and Polynesia. Even within China, themes

BELOW Vase decorated with the animals that represent the 12 months of the year (5th–6th century AD).

and motifs occur in numerous guises. A folktale recorded in Hebei province gives Pangu as the maker of the mud figures that became the first humans. And in another story, the union of Tianlong and Diya, attendants of Wenchang, the God of Literature, gives rise to the first humans. The universality of these motifs seems to indicate the similarity of concerns of people the world over, and the degree to which there is a shared human experience.

The structure of the classical Chinese world is indicated in several sources, and from these it is possible to see that there were a number of cosmographies (theories of the universe). Of the *suan ye* school, very little is known, save that its followers believed the sun and stars moved freely about the heavens. One school held that the universe was in the form of an egg, in which the sky was painted inside the upper part of the shell and the earth floated on the ocean that lay in the lower part of the eggshell. A still older tradition, the *zhou bei* school, held that the sky was an inverted bowl rotating around the axis of the Pole Star; the earth was a square underneath the sky, bordered on each side by one of the four seas. The sky was conceived as a solid dome, supported by four or eight pillars or mountains. The fact that the Pole Star does not occupy a central position in the firmament is ingeniously accounted for in the following myth.

GONGGONG'S DEFEAT

One day the gods Gonggong and Zhurong decided to do battle in order to find out which was the most powerful. After many days of fierce fighting, in the course of which they tumbled right out of the heavens, Gonggong was defeated. He was so ashamed that he resolved to kill himself by running against Mount Buzhou, one of the mountains holding up the sky. The mountain came off much the worse from this encounter, as a great part of it came crashing down. A jagged hole was torn in the sky, and great crevasses appeared in the earth. From these massive chasms fire and water spewed forth, causing a great flood that covered the surface of the earth. Those who escaped drowning saw their crops and homes consumed by the flames. Nugua, who had given these people life, could not bear to see them suffer so, and quickly acted to restore order. She chose some coloured pebbles from the river bed and melted them down into a viscous substance

RIGHT Xiwangmu, Queen Mother of the West, rides on a deer holding a peach and a fungus, both symbols of long life (17th-century soapstone carving).

25

ABOVE *Qing court
robes were embroidered
with dragons, symbols
of imperial authority.*

with which she was able to repair the damage caused to the firmament. In order to be sure that the sky did not collapse again, Nugua slaughtered a giant tortoise and cut off its legs. These she placed at the four points of the compass as extra supports for the heavens. Nugua thus restored order to the world and enabled human beings to carry on their affairs in peace. However, Gonggong's collision with the mountain had caused the heavens to tilt in the direction of the north-west, leaving a void in the south-east. This is the reason all the great rivers of China flow toward the east, empty-ing their waters in that huge ocean.

It is clear that one of the great concerns of Chinese mythology is the maintenance of order and stability. The belief that natural calamities on earth were caused by disharmony in heaven is reiterated many times in the tales of ancient China, although there is only space here for a few of them.

26

CHANG E'S BETRAYAL

A giant mulberry tree called Fusang grew in the sea beyond the eastern ocean, and in this tree dwelt ten suns. These suns, who were the children of Dijun, God of the East, and Xihe, Goddess of the Sun, took it in turns to go out into the sky. Each morning one of the suns would be ferried across the sky in a chariot driven by his mother, thus bringing warmth and light to the world. One day the ten suns rebelled against the routine and all went into the heavens at once, frolicking across the skies. They enjoyed themselves greatly while they brought disaster down below. The earth dried up, causing all the crops to wither, and even the rocks began to melt. Food became scarce and there was hardly anything to drink. In addition, monsters and wild beasts emerged from the forests in search of prey. Dijun and Xihe took pity on suffering humanity and pleaded with their sons to behave, but without success. In exasperation, Dijun summoned the great archer, Yi, and handed him a quiver of white arrows and a red bow.

LEFT *Bronze mirror decorated with Taoist deities; (3rd century* AD)*.*

27

'I depend on you to restore order on earth,' he said. 'Bring my sons under control and slay the wild beasts that are threatening the people.' Yi accepted the challenge and set off, accompanied by his wife, Chang E. It was clear to Yi that he would get nowhere with threats or persuasion so he fitted an arrow to his bow and shot it into the sky. A ball of fire exploded, and the air was filled with golden flames. A moment later, there was a thud as something fell to the ground. People rushed forward and discovered that one of their tormentors had been transformed into a three-legged raven. Yi loosed one arrow after another, each reaching straight to the heart of

BELOW *Earthenware figure of a guardian from a Tang dynasty tomb; (early 8th century* AD).

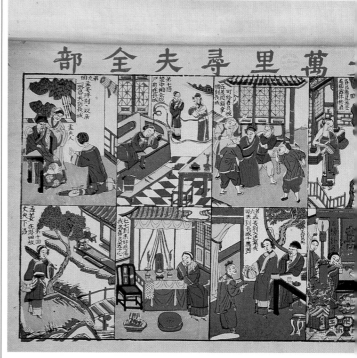

its target. And each time the soul of the sun fell to the ground in the form of a three-legged raven. The air promptly became cooler and, but for the quick thinking of the sage king Yao, all might have been extinguished. Realizing that one sun must remain to provide the earth with light and warmth, Yao counted the number of arrows in Yi's quiver and made sure that Yi would run out before he could shoot down the last sun.

With this task accomplished, Yi now turned his attention to the monsters that still threatened the earth. With great skill and bravery, Yi despatched one fearsome beast after another until at last there was peace.

Yi was looked upon as a great hero and everyone was extremely grateful to him for saving them from a terrible fate. With the sounds of praise still ringing in his ears, Yi returned to heaven with his wife Chang E to report on his successful mission. But instead of welcoming him with open arms, Yi found that the god Dijun had shunned him.

'Although I cannot deny that you have only done my bidding, I find that I cannot bear to look upon you, you who have killed my sons. You and

ABOVE *Early 20th-century New Year woodblock print telling the story of Meng Qiang nu, whose husband was enlisted to build the Great Wall during the Qin dynasty (221–206* BC). *When he failed to return she set off to find him. On hearing that he was among the many who had perished in the course of the construction of the Wall, she began to weep and her tears caused the Wall to collapse. The beginning of the sorry tale is told here, starting on the right-hand side, moving top to bottom.*

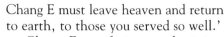

Chang E must leave heaven and return to earth, to those you served so well.'

Chang E was furious at the injustice of this decision, and felt it was particularly unfair that she should be punished for her husband's actions. Reluctantly they packed up their things and moved down to earth.

Yi was able to fill his days with hunting, but Chang E could find no solace in their new home and mulled over their sorry state endlessly. 'Now we have been sent to live in the world of men, and one day, like them, we will die and have to descend to the Underworld. Our only hope is to go to the Queen Mother of the West, who lives on Mount Kunlun, and obtain the elixir of immortality from her.' Yi set off at once and, after many travails, he at last entered the presence of the Queen Mother. The Queen Mother was moved by Yi's sad story and agreed to help him and Chang E.

LEFT *Cakes in the shape of the full harvest moon are eaten during the mid-autumn festival.*

29

ABOVE *Embroidered pillow end showing the hare in the moon under a cassia tree, pounding the elixir of immortality.*

'This box contains enough elixir to give eternal life to two people, although you will still have to remain in the world of men. To obtain complete immortality you would need to take twice as much. Guard the box well, for all I have is contained therein.'

Yi returned home with the precious box and entrusted it to the care of his wife, planning to wait until a suitably auspicious day to take the drug. But Chang E mused, 'Why should I not take the whole amount, and be restored to my former status of goddess.

After all, I have been punished quite without justification.' Immediately after she had taken the elixir, Chang E could feel her feet rise from the ground. Up and up she began to float, out of the window and through the night air.

'On second thoughts,' she said to herself, 'perhaps it would not be such a good idea to return straight to heaven: the gods might criticise me for not sharing the elixir with my husband.'

Chang E resolved to go first to the moon, which was shining overhead in

30

the clear, starlit sky. When she arrived on the moon Chang E found it to be a desolate place, empty except for a hare under a cassia tree. But when she tried to move on, Chang E found that her powers had deserted her and she was doomed to keep her lonely vigil to the end of time.

Yi was shocked and saddened when he found that his wife had betrayed him. He took on a pupil, Peng Meng, perhaps hoping that his skills at least would not die with him. Peng Meng studied hard and eventually reached the point where only Yi was better than him at archery. Peng Meng grew increasingly jealous of his master's superiority, and one day, in an opportune moment, killed him.

A very popular and well-known myth concerning stars in the sky is that of the ox herd and the weaving girl, who respectively represent the stars Altair and Vega, on either side of the Milky Way. This story holds particular significance for parted lovers; indeed, a husband and wife who have been assigned to work in different parts of the country are referred to in such terms.

ABOVE *Embroidered pillow end showing Chang E on her flight to the moon.*

31

THE PARTED LOVERS

A poor young peasant lad just managed to make a living from his barren soil with the help of his most valued possession, his ox. He was honest, worked hard and was liked and respected by all, but the young man felt his life was empty without a wife and family. One day his ox revealed to his owner that he was in fact the Ox Star, sent to earth as a punishment for wrongdoing. 'As you have treated me kindly, I will reward you by helping you to find a wife.'

The Ox Star told the young man to go the next day and hide himself in the undergrowth surrounding a nearby pool, which he said was used by the Heavenly Maidens to bathe in. Following his instructions, the ox herd hid by the pool of clear water, and sure enough, before long a group of beautiful young girls arrived at the water's edge. They left their bright clothes on the bank and stepped into the water. While the girls were occupied with their toilette, the ox herd hid the pile of clothes that was nearest him. As the girls emerged from the water, the young man came out from his hiding place, causing the girls to panic, and grabbing their clothes, they flew off into the sky. One could not find her garments and was trapped on the ground, terrified. But when the young man spoke to her kindly, she realized he meant her no harm and agreed to be his wife. After their marriage, she divulged that she was in fact the granddaughter of heaven and the goddess of weaving. Thanks to the wife's skills, their fortunes pros-

32

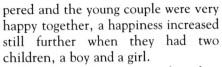

pered and the young couple were very happy together, a happiness increased still further when they had two children, a boy and a girl.

But the gods were not pleased at the thought of the weaving maid remaining on earth and sent down messengers to snatch her back to her rightful abode. The ox herd and his children watched helplessly as the weaving maid was carried, weeping, back to heaven. The old ox came once more to the aid of his master: 'I shall die soon, and when I do, you must take my skin and wrap yourself in it, then you will be able to pursue your wife.' The ox herd did as he was told, and then, placing his children in two baskets suspended from a carrying pole across his shoulders, he set off.

The ox herd soon caught sight of

BELOW *Pagoda of the Six Harmonies, West Lake, Hangzhou; popular belief holds that building a pagoda will bring good luck to a place.*

his wife, but, before he could reach her, he was spotted by her grandfather, or some say, her grandmother, Xiwangmu, the Queen Mother of the West. A line drawn in the sky became a raging torrent, running between them. The little girl urged her father to use the ladle he had placed in the basket with her as ballast to empty the water from the river. The sight of the devoted family at their hopeless task touched the hearts of the gods, and it was decided that the family could be united once a year. On the seventh day of the seventh month, all the magpies fly up from earth and form a bridge across the river, enabling the ox herd to cross over and visit his wife. Some say that when rain falls on this day, it is the tears of the weaving maid as she weeps tears of joy.

The festival that is held on this date is the annual feast of young girls,

in which they entreat the weaving goddess to give them skills in spinning, weaving and embroidery. It is said that the ladies of the Tang Emperor Xuan Zong would shut a spider into a box on this night, and take the web found the following day to be an indication of the skill of the one who imprisoned it.

Throughout the history of China, countless numbers of people have lived alongside the great rivers, the Yangtse and the Yellow River, knowing that the waters that provided them with the means of irrigating their fields could also one day deprive them of their life and livelihood. Although the deluge motif occurs in numerous myths the world over, it assumes a particular significance in Chinese mythology. The following tales illustrate the importance of controlling flood waters, and the degree of respect accorded to those who had such powers.

ABOVE *The transplanting of rice seedlings is carried out today in the same back-breaking fashion as it has been for centuries; the overwhelming importance of a good harvest informs many of the myths of China.*

RIGHT *17th-century Ming dynasty ivory figure of the Taoist immortal, Chang Kuo Lao.*

THE GREAT FLOOD

During the reign of the sage king Yao, Tiandi, the supreme god in heaven, sent a terrible flood down to earth to punish mankind for its wickedness. The waters covered the fields and villages, and people were forced to seek refuge in the mountains. They had to compete with wild animals for food and shelter and their suffering was very great. Of all the gods in heaven, only one took pity on the plight of those on earth, and his name was Gun. Gun felt that the punishment meted out was too severe and pleaded with Tiandi to end the deluge. But his entreaties were in vain.

One day, when he was racking his brains trying to think of a way to control the flood water, Gun came across an owl and a tortoise. When Gun told them of his concern, the owl and the tortoise replied, 'Tiandi has a magical substance, which looks just like an ordinary lump of earth. If you could get hold of a piece of this substance and throw it into the water, it would swell up into great barriers that would hold back the flood.'

Gun's determination to save the people was so great that he managed to overcome all obstacles and obtain a

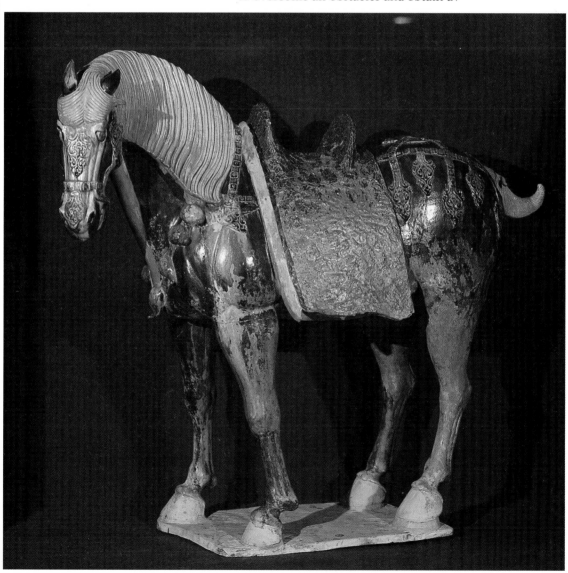

RIGHT *Glazed earthenware tomb figure of a horse from the Tang dynasty (7th–10th century* AD*).*

35

small piece of the magic soil. He immediately set off for earth and dropped a tiny lump into the water. At once, the soil started to heave and shift below the surface, and before long the tips of ridges and mountains could be seen. The flood waters were soon contained by these formations, and then dried up completely. The people were overcome with gratitude for Gun's actions, and danced and sang his praises. But Tiandi was furious when he discovered what Gun had done and sent the fire god Zhurong down to earth to seek revenge. Zhurong killed Gun and took what remained of the magic soil back to heaven, and floods again covered the world.

Although Gun had been killed, his spirit refused to die because he had not accomplished his task. New life began to grow inside his body, which would not decompose. After three years had passed, during which the

mourning people had kept watch over the body of their saviour, Tiandi sent down a god with a sword to destroy Gun's remains. When the blade slashed at Gun's body, a terrible dragon was released. This dragon was none other than the Great Yu, Gun's son, who took on his father's unfinished mission and eventually brought the flood under control. Gun himself then turned into a yellow dragon and went to live at the bottom of the sea.

Dragons are the most important of all the mythical beasts to be found in the Chinese tradition. In contrast to western notions, Chinese dragons were believed to be generally well-disposed towards humankind, although subject to rather short tempers! Dragons represent the male *yang* element. From the Han dynasty on, the dragon was used as a symbol of the Son of Heaven, the emperor. The phoenix correspondingly represented the female *yin*, and the empress – together the dragon

RIGHT *Phoenixes dancing amid peonies and rocks; 16th–17th-century silk tapestry.*

RIGHT *18th-century porcelain figure of a phoenix, symbol of the empress.*

and the phoenix are used to indicate a state of marital harmony.

There is a particular affinity between dragons and water in all its natural forms: seas, rivers, lakes, rain. Four dragon-kings were believed to rule over the four seas that surround the earth, and dragon-kings could also be found in lakes and rivers inhabiting crystal palaces filled with precious treasure. Dragons were held to exercise control over rainfall, and are often depicted playing with a ball or pearl (symbol of thunder) among the rainclouds.

At the beginning of the Chinese year according to the lunar calendar, some time in February, a dragon dance is performed. A line of dancers each hold a stick supporting a section of the dragon's body, from head to tail. A lead dancer holds a lantern in the shape of a red ball. By moving up and down and back and forth, the dancers give the impression that the dragon is writhing around in pursuit of the ball.

This dance, which may have originated in an ancient ritual to do with the preparation of the soil before the spring sowing, is performed by Chinese communities throughout the world. The dragon-boat festival of South China is held on the fifth day of the fifth month of the lunar calender (around the middle of June). Teams of men in long, narrow boats with dragon-shaped prows compete in a rowing race. The loss of a rower overboard was held to be a sacrifice to the dragon-god, and since many Chinese could not swim, this was a not unusual occurrence.

It was widely believed that the landscape was criss-crossed with 'dragon-lines', veins of the earth. Before building a house or choosing a burial site, people would consult a geomancer to ascertain whether the proposed development was likely to obstruct the natural forces flowing through the dragon lines, thus arousing the dragon's anger and causing

RIGHT *Chinese communities the world over perform the dragon dance at New Year in the Chinese calendar.*

38

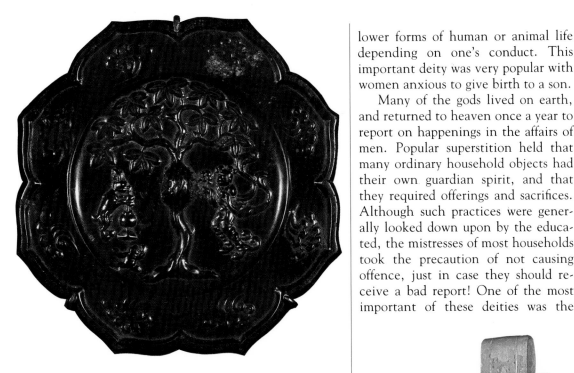

ABOVE *Tang dynasty bronze mirror showing Chang E under the cassia tree with the hare that inhabits the moon.*

lower forms of human or animal life depending on one's conduct. This important deity was very popular with women anxious to give birth to a son.

Many of the gods lived on earth, and returned to heaven once a year to report on happenings in the affairs of men. Popular superstition held that many ordinary household objects had their own guardian spirit, and that they required offerings and sacrifices. Although such practices were generally looked down upon by the educated, the mistresses of most households took the precaution of not causing offence, just in case they should receive a bad report! One of the most important of these deities was the

calamity. So strong are these beliefs that geomancers are regularly employed even in somewhere as relentlessly 20th century as Hong Kong. Although officially regarded as pedlars of feudal superstitious nonsense in China today, geomancers continue to advise, particularly in the countryside.

Chinese people believed that there was a great deal of communication between heaven and earth. In fact, heaven was generally conceived as reflecting the organization of society below: the emperor, who stood at the head of a vast bureaucracy, had his counterpart above, Shangdi. As on earth, Shangdi was served by numerous functionaries and officials. The supreme ruler, who was also known simply as Tian, or 'sky', appears in his Taoist guise as the Jade Emperor. An important functionary in the heavenly pantheon was the Jade Emperor's deputy, who headed an office concerned with all matters of life and death on earth. The officials in this ministry fixed the times of birth and death, determining the span of life of both human and animal life. This accorded with the Buddhist idea of reincarnation, in which one's soul can be reborn many times in higher or

LEFT *The dead were buried with all they might need in the afterlife, including attendants (Tang dynasty).*

39

kitchen, or hearth god. A statue or image of this god would be kept in a niche above the stove and during the course of the year, he would keep watch over the comings and goings in the house. At New Year, to ensure that he was in a good temper before his journey back to heaven, he would be offered a good meal and his lips were smeared with honey so that he could only utter sweet words. Then, to the accompaniment of fire-crackers, the soot-blackened image would be burnt to send it on its way. Like many other Chinese gods, the hearth god was thought to have originally been a human being. One story tells that he

RIGHT *Guandi, the God of War, also epitomized justice. Parties involved in a legal dispute would present their case at temples dedicated to him.*

was a poor mason, in such straits that he was no longer able to support his wife. Forced to give her in marriage to another, he took to wandering the countryside, begging. By chance, he came one day to the house where his former wife lived. Overcome with shame, he tried to escape by climbing into the hearth, little realizing that it was alight. After his painful death, he was made into a god.

Many of the popular Chinese gods were historical characters with outstanding qualities who were deified after death. One of these was Guandi, the God of War, in whose name numerous temples and shrines were dedicated. Guan Zhong, as he was known in his lifetime, was one of a band of three brigands who lived at the end of the Late Han dynasty, a

ABOVE *Qing dynasty print of a door god with the gods of wealth and acolytes.*

RIGHT *Qing dynasty New Year print of the Kitchen God.*

40

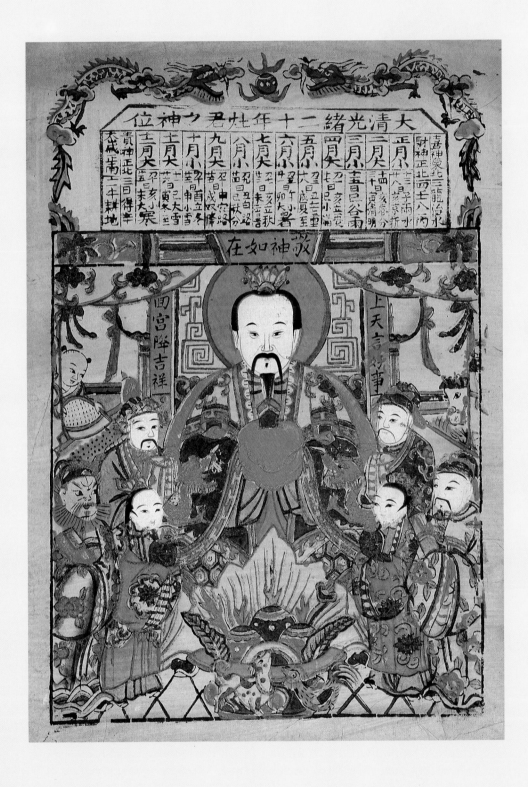

ABOVE *Gilt bronze statue of Bodhisattva sitting on a lotus leaf, a Buddhist deity who stayed in the world in order to save others; (Liao dynasty, 907–1125 AD).*

Chinese everywhere is Guan Yin, the goddess of mercy, who was originally the male Buddhist Boddhisatva, Avalokitsvara. This saint, whose name translated into Chinese means 'one who hears the cries of the world', is also the patron saint of Tibetan Buddhism. Guan Yin is often portrayed as a madonna with a child in her arms, and is worshipped by those hoping for a child. Fishermen consider her to keep particular watch over those in peril at sea, and she is sometimes identified with Mazu, whose cult has spread out from the coastal regions of south China. There are images of Guan Yin not only in temples and shrines, but also in homes and public places; her figure has been executed in all manner of media – she is the most revered of all gods in the popular pantheon. The following story indicates the degree of affection she inspires.

THE GIFT OF RICE

In the time when people lived by hunting and gathering, life was very hard and uncertain. When Guan Yin saw how people suffered and often died from starvation, she was moved to help them. She squeezed her breasts so that milk flowed and with this she filled the ears of the rice plant. In order to adequately provide for the people, she produced such quantities that her milk became mixed with blood towards the end. This is why there are two kinds of rice – white and red.

An alternative myth gives a dog the credit for introducing rice. After the great floods had been brought under control by Yu, son of Gun, people were forced to live by hunting as all the old plants had been washed away. One day a dog ran out of a waterlogged field and was found to be carrying long ears of rice that had got caught up in his tail. When the seeds were planted in the sodden fields they

period of great turmoil. The story of his life is recounted in *The Romance of the Three Kingdoms*, which was written at the beginning of the Ming dynasty although it purports to be a contemporary account of events, and it has been the inspiration for many plays and novels since. Guan Zhong first achieved renown for his military prowess, but came to be loved for great courage and loyalty. Guandi is instantly recognizable, as he is always portrayed with a red face.

The deity held most dear by the

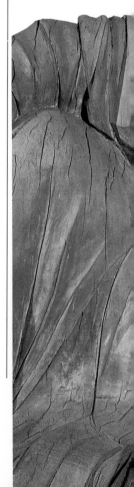

grew and ripened. In gratitude, the first meal after the rice harvest is shared with the dog.

Of all the animals that occur in Chinese myths, both real and fantastic, Monkey is in a class of his own. His story is related in *Xi you ji*, or *Journey to the West*, written by Wu Cheng'en in the 16th century. This novel purports to be a true account of the travels of the Buddhist monk Xuan Zang, who journeyed to India in the 7th century in search of Buddhist sutras. He returned to China after an absence of 16 years and spent the rest of his life translating the 520 cases of texts he had brought back with him. In the book, Tripitaka (as Xuan Zang is named after the Buddhist scriptures he seeks) is accompanied by Monkey and Pigsy, two creatures who have no

LEFT *18th century woodblock edition of* Journey to the West *by Wu Cheng'en. Monkey is at the top, the monk Tripitaka to the right and Pigsy centre left.*

historical basis whatsoever. Although Monkey has many wonderful and supernatural powers, and a sense of mischief and a temper to match, Pigsy is a completely down-to-earth character, who epitomizes the coarser human desires.

MONKEY'S IMMORTALITY

Monkey was born from a stone egg that had rested on the side of the Aolai Mountain in the Eastern sea ever since Pangu had created the world. Although in appearance there was nothing to distinguish this monkey from others, he was in fact possessed of magical powers. The tribe of monkeys with whom he lived recognized his special qualities and adopted him as their king. After he had been king for about 300 years, Monkey began to concern himself with the eventual fate that he and his tribe faced. He decided to seek the way of immortality

BELOW *Life-size carved wooden figure of a Buddhist* lohan, *an enlightened holy man,* *(14th century).*

that he had heard of through the tales of the Buddha and other deities. So Monkey left the mountain and travelled to the world of men. Here he found a master who agreed to take him on as a disciple. According to custom, Monkey was given a new name – Sun, the enlightened one, since *sun* is the Chinese word for monkey. After 20 years not only had Monkey learnt the secret of eternal life, but he had also acquired other valuable skills, such as the ability to change himself into any form, and fly through the air.

When Monkey returned to Aolai mountain, he found that a demon monster had taken over the monkeys' home. After defeating the monster in battle, Monkey decided he needed to

BELOW *16th-century stoneware figure of a judge of Hell.*

get hold of a good magic weapon. He called on the Dragon King of the Eastern Sea, and against the dragon's will, carried off an iron pillar that had been used by the Great Yu, controller of the floods. The size of this pillar could be changed by its owner in an instant, so it could be made as small as a needle to be carried about and then turned at once into an eight-foot-long fighting staff.

One day, as he was feasting and drinking in the company of his fellow monkeys, Monkey was approached by two messengers from the Underworld. When they refused to take heed of his protest that he had become an immortal, Monkey became extremely angry. Laying about him with his magic cudgel, he knocked down his would-be guards, and charged off into the Underworld in a fury. The officials and judges at the courts of Hell were soon beaten into submission by the

ABOVE *Qing dynasty porcelain vase decorated in* famille rose *enamels. Peaches are credited with the power to ward off evil spirits, as well as being a symbol of immortality.*

44

furious Monkey. He demanded to see the Register of the Dead, and on finding his own entry 'Soul no. 1735, Sun the enlightened one: 342 years and a peaceful death', flew into a further rage. Monkey snatched up a brush and crossed out the lines referring to himself and his tribe. Throwing the book on to the floor, Monkey stormed out and returned to his mountain fastness.

However, news of Monkey's exploits was beginning to reach the ears of the great Jade Emperor. Both the Dragon King of the Eastern Sea and Yama, Lord of the Underworld, made complaints about Monkey's arrogant behaviour. It was decided that it would be a good idea to bring Monkey up to

heaven where he could be kept under supervision. Monkey was offered the post of 'Keeper of the Heavenly Horses', and, thinking this was an important post in the heavenly bureaucracy, he duly accepted. After a short period in the job, Monkey started to make enquiries about his grade and salary and flew into a terrible rage when he discovered that his was an honorary post that carried no salary and was too lowly to figure in the heavenly hierarchy. The only way to persuade the proud Monkey to stay in heaven was to offer him the grand title 'Great Sage, equal of Heaven' (which sounded important but was in fact meaningless). After a time during which Monkey did nothing but amuse himself feasting and drinking with his friends, he was given the job of guardian of the Garden of Immortal Peaches in a desperate attempt to keep him out of trouble.

This garden belonged to Xiwangmu, Queen Mother of the West, and, every 6,000 years, when the fruit ripened, she would hold a great feast to which the immortals were invited in order to partake of the peaches and renew their immortality. It so happened that the peaches were nearly ripe and, of course, Monkey could not resist plucking one to see what it tasted like. It was so delicious that he ate one after another, until eventually he fell asleep in the branches of one of the trees. He was woken by a maid who had been sent to pick the peaches in preparation for the Queen Mother's banquet. Monkey was apoplectic when he learnt that he was not to be invited to the celebrations, and determined to seek revenge for being slighted. He had already eaten most of the ripe peaches in the garden and now proceeded to down great quantities of the fragrant wine that had been prepared for the feast. And when he came across gourds containing the elixir of immortality which Laozi was intending to bring to the occasion, well, he drank that too.

After a while, when he had sobered up a little, Monkey began to realize

LEFT *Ming ivory figurine of an attendant to Xiwangmu, Queen Mother of the West, holding three peaches of immortality.*

金剛般若波羅蜜經

奉請紫賢金剛
奉請白淨水金剛
奉請除災金剛
循唎 循唎 摩訶循唎 循循唎
般若讀經光念淨口業真言 遍

奉請大神金剛
奉請紫嚴金剛
奉請辟妻金剛
奉請黃隨求金剛
婆婆訶
奉請定陳尼金剛

the enormity of the offence he had just committed. Feeling some remorse, he returned to the mountain and hid in his old home. The gods were livid when it was discovered what Monkey had done, and determined to punish him. After many great struggles, Monkey was brought before the Jade Emperor, bound hand and foot. Monkey could not be sentenced to death because he had consumed so many immortality-conferring substances, so it was decided that he should be burnt in Laozi's crucible. But 49 days of white-hot heat merely gave Monkey red rims to his eyes, and he leapt from the crucible ready to continue to do battle.

In desperation, the Jade Emperor called on Buddha himself for help.

Buddha was amused by the antics of the insolent Monkey and, placing him in the palm of his giant hand, issued him with a challenge. 'If you can leap out of my hand, you can rule over heaven. If not, you must return to earth and work to achieve immortality.'

Monkey took a great leap into the air and hurled himself into the distance. When he landed on the ground at last, he found himself at the foot of a great mountain. Monkey plucked out one of his hairs and used it as a brush to write his name on the rocks. Then he urinated on the ground, like animals do to mark out their territory, before returning to Buddha. When Monkey claimed his right to be ruler of heaven, since he had been to the

46

ends of the earth and back, Buddha burst out laughing,

'You never even left my hand! See, here is your name written on one of my fingers.' Monkey saw that there was no way he would ever be able to outwit Buddha, and tried to escape. But Buddha quickly created a mountain and imprisoned Monkey inside it, saying, 'There you will stay until you have paid for your sins'.

Five hundred years later, after Guanyin's intercession on his behalf, Monkey is released from his prison on the condition that he accompany the monk Tripitaka on his great journey to the West, and protect him from harm. The two travellers pick up a third companion, Pigsy, as they continue their dangerous and eventful journey, and after surviving 14 years and 80 perils, the little band finally come in sight of the Buddha's abode, the Mountain of the Soul. When they have received the scriptures from the Buddha himself, the three set off on their journey home. Thanks to Guanyin, this time they are able to travel in comfort, riding on a cloud borne by one of the Golden Guardians. This is brought abruptly to an end when Buddha decides they should face one more test, bringing the total trials they have undergone to the magic number of 81, nine times nine.

The three companions suddenly find themselves tumbling down to earth. On picking themselves up they recognize the spot as being the bank of a river they had crossed on their

RIGHT *Papercut image of Monkey about to eat a peach; his fur is covered with flowers, coins and swastikas, the latter a symbol of good luck in both India and China.*

ABOVE *This page from
a contemporary comic
book telling the
Monkey story indicates
the enduring popularity
of the tale.*

outward journey on the back of a white turtle. The turtle appears to ferry them across again but, in mid-stream, enquires whether Tripitaka has indeed found out from the Buddha the life span of a turtle, a task that he undertook on their previous meeting. In the excitement of coming before the Buddha, Tripitaka had in fact completely forgotten about the turtle's query. On learning this, the turtle is so cross that he promptly tips them all into the water. Fortunately, they manage to swim to shore with their precious cargo, where they are received with great joy by the local people. On reaching the capital, Chang'an, they are brought before the emperor in a majestic ceremony. The three receive their final accolade in heaven, when Buddha announces that Tripitaka was once his disciple, who was sent to earth in punishment for his sins. Now Tripitaka is to be permitted to take up his place at the Buddha's side again, Monkey is made God of Victorious Battle, and Pigsy is created Chief Heavenly Altar Cleaner.

The story of Monkey has been portrayed in every medium – book, play, opera, film – and continues to be greatly enjoyed by Chinese audiences. Monkey's mischievous antics and skill at martial arts delight people today as they have done for centuries.

Although China has such a long written history, there are difficulties for the student of mythology. As in the case of the *Journey to the West*, many texts are not as old as they purport to be, with material selectively incorporated by their authors in order to give credence to their own accounts. Often, the same basic myth exists in a number of variations, there is no one single authorized version. The *Shanhaijing*, the Mountain and Seas Classic, edited in the 1st century BC, and the *Huainanzi*, the writings of Marter Huai Nan, compiled in the 2nd century BC, are both rich sources of classical myths. During the Tang dynasty, one of the most artistically creative periods of Chinese history, there was much interest in magic and the supernatural, and themes from

BELOW *Actors in
Peking opera apply
their own make-up.
The patterns and
colours all have a
particular significance.*

early myth and folklore were woven into stories written at this time.

The different contributions made to Chinese mythology by Confucianism, Taoism and Buddhism have already been indicated; it is worth remembering that the area of China covers a great variety of cultural and linguistic traditions. Han Chinese, who constitute 94 per cent of the one billion population of the People's Republic today, are only one of the 50 or so ethnolinguistic groupings identified within China's boundaries.

This diverse heritage has given rise to a body of stories that is a rich and vital part of Chinese life. It is impossible to make sense of Chinese literature without a knowledge of its myths, for they are constantly referred to. Today these tales are still the subject of numerous retellings – in book and comic form, or as plays, opera or even film. In festivals and holidays, in painting and sculpture, as figures of speech, the myths of ancient China live on in the lives of ordinary Chinese people everywhere.

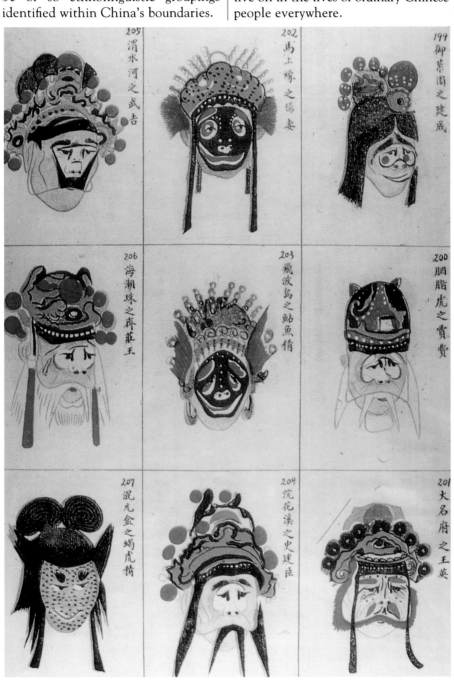

RIGHT *Designs for face make-up used in Chinese theatre; each design is for a specific character or type of character.*

49

Indian Mythology

All over India millions of tiny oil lamps are lit as dusk falls. They shine out, row upon row of them, from rooftops and windowsills. It is autumn, the night of the great festival of Diwali. Children settle down around their mothers or grandmothers to hear the story of Lakshmi, the fickle goddess of wealth and good fortune. Hearing this tale, and countless others, at their mother's knee is their entertainment. They are absorbed in a rich fantasy world of gods and demons, princes and princesses, friendly animals and exciting adventures. Their psyches have free range over ideas of good and evil, exploring ways of living life and of facing death. They find these stories in books, films, theatre, dance, sculpture and painting, and in comics, but nothing compares with the power of an ancient tale directly told, handed down by word of mouth from generation to generation for thousands of years.

Vishnu, the most popular of the Hindu deities, and his consort, Lakshmi, ride on the bird-god Garuda; (18th-century Bundi painting from Rajasthan).

There is always a moral to the story: how to be the perfect wife or husband, how to be reborn as a better person, how to behave toward others, how to keep the gods happy with sacrifice and celebration. Much of Indian mythology holds a religious context, which speaks .in particular to those holy men and women, priests, hermits and wandering ascetics who are searching for the key to the ultimate nature of reality, and for the way to escape the endless cycle of rebirth.

For the historian, the language and images of the ancient mythological texts present the ancient history of the land. The migrations of the Aryan peoples into India can be followed by tracing the burial and cremation practices of the region, as described in the ancient Vedic hymns. The cultural influences of the indigenous Dravidian peoples can be seen in the increased importance of the goddesses in subsequent sacred texts. The struggles of rival dynasties are vividly described in the great battles of the epic poems, the *Ramayana* and the *Mahabharata*. Indeed, Indian mythology is like a mirror that shows their hearts' desire to all who look into it.

Most of the stories in this introduction are Hindu tales, but other religions have not been overlooked. The story of the life of the Buddha, for example, is included. Although he is an historical figure, his life itself has been turned into an elaborate myth involving gods and demons, even though the Buddhist doctrine is atheistic. The Buddha is even sometimes described as an incarnation of Vishnu.

In the Indian Hindu tradition, the lives of famous holy men, saints, and the founders of other great religions are elaborated in similar ways. For instance, Mahavira, the founder of Jainism, was born after his mother had a visionary dream. The astrologers forecast his coming and the gods closely observed his young life full of heroic feats.

Traditional biographers also elaborated the life of the founder of Sik-

hism, Guru Nanak, who lived from 1469 to 1539. Although he believed in only one God, his birth was said to be witnessed by millions of gods who foretold his future as a great man. This greatness is exhibited in various feats of magic. For example, when his disciple Mardana was hungry, Guru Nanak turned poison berries into edible fruits. The story of his enlightenment is that he disappeared while bathing in the river and was presumed dead. After three days he returned and explained that he had been with God. His first words on his return were said to be 'There is neither Hindu or Muslim, so whose path shall I fol-

BELOW *The Jain saint Parsvanartha; (11th-century sculpture from Orissa). The austerity of Jain doctrine is expressed in the simple, continuous form.*

low? I will follow God's path. God is neither Hindu nor Muslim, and the path I follow is God's'. But even in the *Adi Granth*, or Original Collection of the hymns of the Gurus, the one God is sometimes described with reference to the Hindu deities: 'He, the One, is Himself Brahma, Vishnu and Shiva'.

Similarly, the animal stories of the Buddhist Jataka tales use all kinds of folk tales that have been used to illustrate Buddhist values. Some of these tales have been floating around the world for centuries and turn up in different forms in Homer, Boccaccio and Chaucer. They can be claimed by anyone! (Some students of Indian

LEFT *A Jain saint in the arms of his mother; (11th-century stone icon from western India).*

53

mythology believe that Hinduism claimed the epic poems of the *Ramayana* and the *Mahabharata* in the same way by inserting sacred texts, such as the *Bhaghavad Gita*, at appropriate points in the story.)

'Each myth celebrates the belief that the universe is boundlessly various, that everything occurs simultaneously, that all possibilities may exist without excluding each other' (Wendy O'Flaherty, *The Origins of Evil in Indian Mythology*). This is also a good way to describe the Indian subcontinent itself. It is geographically diverse, with the great Himalayan mountains in the north, rice- and wheat-growing plains, desert and tropical jungle, high, tea-growing plateaux and low-lying coastal areas with palm trees where the land is criss-crossed with waterways. The climate is extreme, the hot season brought to an abrupt end by the heavy monsoon rains. Although 8 out of 10 Indians are Hindus, India is the home of many followers of other great world religions, including Islam and Christianity.

IN THE BEGINNING

Some of the creation myths are very abstract, struggling with the concepts of existence and non-existence as in this extract from the hymn of creation from the *Rig Veda*.

'Neither not-being nor being was there at that time; there was no air-filled space nor was there the sky which is beyond it. What enveloped all? And where? Under whose protection? What was the unfathomable deep water? . . . Upon it rose up, in the beginning, desire, which was the mind's first seed. Having sought in their hearts, the wise ones discovered, through deliberation, the bond of being and nonbeing . . . Whereupon this creation has issued, whether he has made it or whether he has not –

he who is the superintendent of this world in the highest heaven – he alone knows, or, perhaps, even he does not know.'

There are other stories where the gods actively create the world. The story of Prajapati, who rose from the primordial waters weeping as he was lonely and did not know why he had been born, for example. The tears that fell into the water became the earth, the tears that he wiped away became the sky and the air. Then he created people and spirits, night and day, the seasons and finally death.

In a creation myth using the concept of the egg – also found in Chinese and many many other mythologies – Brahma is the creator. The golden egg grew from a seed floating on the cosmic ocean for a year, and shone with the lustre of the sun. Brahma emerged from the egg and split himself into two people, one male and one female, the incestuous union of these two being the creative force. Brahma is also called Narayana (he who came from the waters) who is described as lying on a banyan leaf, floating on primeval waters sucking his toe – a symbol of eternity.

One fascinating creation myth

ABOVE *Three-headed icon of Brahma, the creator; early 11th-century Chola sculpture from south India.*

RIGHT *The Cosmic Egg according to Hindu theory; 18th-century painting (gouache on paper) from Rajasthan. At the bottom is Vishnu, reclining on the cosmic serpent. From his navel protrudes the lotus upon which sits Brahma. At the top is Vaikuntha, or paradise, where Krishna dwells.*

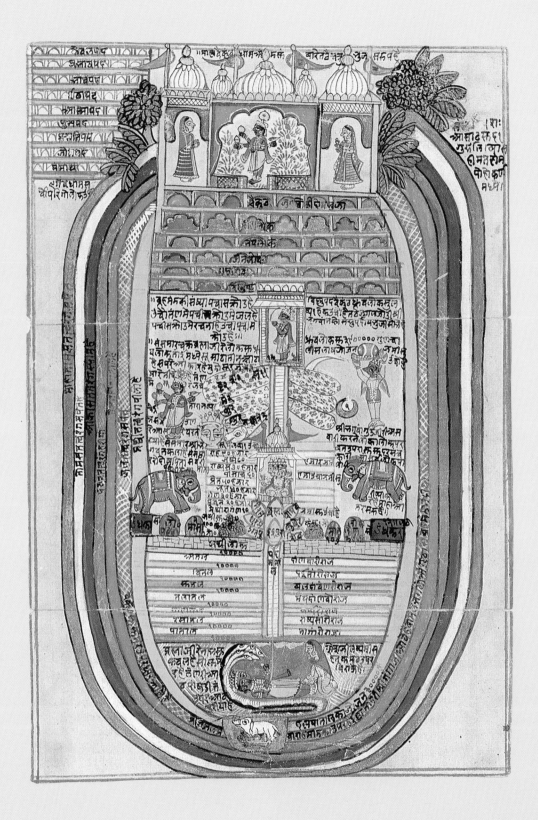

involves the sacrifice of Purusha, the cosmic person. The description of the sacrifice evokes the ritualistic atmosphere of the worship and the way in which the body of the victim is divided up is said to be the origin of the caste system. This is a translation of some of the verses of the Hymn to the Cosmic Person. It is part of the *Rig Veda,* the earliest book of the songs of the ancient seers which was composed by the Vedic Aryans who came into India from central Asia. They overran the already established Indus Valley civilization. The Vedic period spans approximately 2500 to 600 BC.

Indra was the most prominent god in the *Rig Veda.* He is identified with

RIGHT *Agni, the Vedic god of Fire; 11th-century bronze from Orissa.*

thunder and wields the *vajra* or thunderbolt, and his most significant deed is the slaying of the demon Vritra who holds captive the sun and the rain. This deed can be seen to represent either the conquest of India by Aryan warriors led by their champion, Indra; or as the cosmological allegory of the conquest of chaos and the release of the life forces of water, heat and light.

Agni is second only to Indra in the Vedic pantheon. He is the personification and deification of fire. His three forms are terrestial as fire, atmospheric as lightning, and celestial as the sun. He is a messenger between mortals and the gods and therefore particularly important as the sacrificial fire.

A thousand headed is the cosmic
person.
With a thousand eyes and feet,
Enveloping the earth on all sides,
And going ten fingers beyond.

When they divided the cosmic person,
Into how many parts did they divide
him?
What did they call his mouth? What
his arms?
What did they call his legs? What his
feet?
His mouth was the priestly class,

ABOVE *Impression of a Steatite seal from Mohenjo-Daro showing a humped Brahmani bull (Indus valley civilization c. 2500–2000 BC). Seals like this one are the earliest art objects in India. Less than 2ins (4cms) high, the fine craftsmanship betrays a keen observation of animal form. Frequent portrayal of bulls on such seals suggest that they were religious symbols.*

RIGHT *Putusa, the thousand-headed cosmic person, standing on Vishnu; 17th-century Nepali painting (gouache on cloth).*

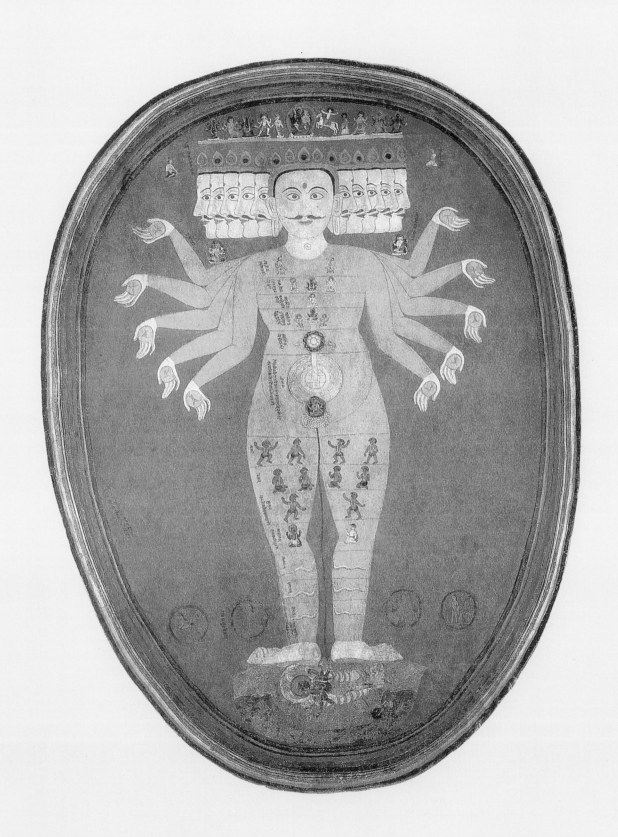

The sky came from his head.
From his feet came earth, from his
    ears the four regions.
Thus they formed the worlds.

(John M. Koller, *The Indian Way*)

His arms the warrior-princes.
His legs were the producers,
His feet the servant class.

From his mind was born the moon,
From his eye was born the sun.
Indra and Agni came from his mouth,
And the wind was born of his breath

From his navel came the atmosphere,

MEASURING THE COSMOS

The legend which provides the key to Hindu cosmology and introduces us to the cyclical theory of time and to the theory of the transmigration of souls is the myth of the four Ages of Man.

The four Ages, or Yugas, are named after four throws of the dice. The Krita Yuga was the perfect age when there were no gods or demons, people were saintly and there was no disease. The Treta Yuga was when sacrifices began and virtue lessened a quarter. The Dwapara Yuga was a decadent age when virtue lessened one half and there came desire, disease and calamities. And the Kali Yuga is the degenerate age when only one quarter of virtue remains and people are wicked. The latter is, of course, the age that we live in.

The ancient mathematicians worked out that these four ages spread over 4,320,000 years, and that 1,000 of these periods equals one day of Brahma. At the end of each 'day' (*kalpa*), Brahma sleeps for a night of equal length, and before he falls asleep the universe is destroyed by fire and flood and becomes as it was in the beginning. He creates anew when he wakes the next morning. A year of Brahma is 360 *kalpas* and he endures for 100 years – and that is half of his existence. After another 100 years of chaos and disorder, a new Brahma will arise to create a new universe, and so the cycle will begin again.

This eternal cycle of creation and destruction is the backdrop to the eternal cycle of birth and death that those who believe in reincarnation

THE SPREAD OF BUDDHISM

The painting below is from a 19th-century Burmese book of illustrations of Buddhist heavens and hells. Buddhism has evolved according to national cultures to a bewildering extent: the Zen Buddhism of Japan, the Lamaistic Buddhism of Tibet, and Burmese and Sri Lankan Buddhism all have different emphases, Buddhist sects having quickly sprung up after the fifth century BC, basing their philosophies upon specific scriptures. Thus Zen Buddhism is based upon meditation in order to achieve 'sudden enlightenment', while Tibetan Buddhism, which arrived in the country and flourished in the 7th century AD, emphasizes the practices of the Tantra. Buddhism is divided into two main schools: the Theravada, or Hinayana, which predominates in Sri Lanka, Burma and Southeast Asia, and the Mahayana, found in China, Korea and Japan. A chief distinction is the Mahayana veneration of the Bodhisattva, a person who refuses to enter nirvana and escape the cycle of death and rebirth – even though he has earned the right – until all others have been similarly enlightened and saved.

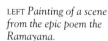

nature. Belief in a creator is considered an evil doctrine and makes no sense because '. . . If he were transcendant he would not create, for he would be free; nor if involved in transmigration, for then he would not be almighty.' (*Sources of Indian Tradition* ed. T. de Bary)

Although the great ascetic philosophy of Jainism rejected much of Hindu thought, the two beliefs shared one vision of the cosmos. The emphasis Jains laid on wisdom and teaching preserved and created many important learned texts on mathematics and other objects and also formed a body of popular literature in many different Indian languages. They have produced many beautiful maps of the cosmos, full of measurements and fine details.

Brahma, Shiva and Vishnu are the three most important of the Hindu gods. Brahma, the creator, is not worshipped as a personal god today and there is only one temple dedicated to him in the whole of India. His wife is Sarasvati, the goddess of learning and the patroness of arts, sciences and speech. Her earthly embodiment is the river Sarasvati, and as the river she presides over religious festivals

BELOW *Ephemeral clay figures of Sarasvati, the goddess of learning, wisdom, eloquence, music and the arts. She carries a Vina (a stringed instrument) and is mounted on a swan. During worship the clay figurines are carried in procession through the streets and then immersed in the Ganges or a nearby river or tank. Sarasvati is a popular deity in Bengal.*

must endure. The atheistic Jains reject the doctrines of a divine creator. For them natural laws provide a more satisfactory explanation. They believe that the world is not created but is without beginning or end, existing under the compulsion of its own

LEFT *Stone icon of Harihari, or Shiva and Vishnu combined, (c. 1000 AD).*

61

and gives fertility and wisdom to the earth. She may be portrayed holding the stringed instrument, the *vina,* a lotus bud, a book, a rosary, a drum or a stick of sugar cane.

Shiva is a very ancient god. He is still extremely popular today and is often worshipped in the form of a *lingam,* a stone phallus. He represents the underlying unity of existence in which all opposites are reconciled. He is creator and destroyer. As Lord of the Dance he dances out the awesome rhythms of creation and destruction, but as well as being a bringer of death, he conquers death and disease and is invoked to cure sickness. He is the great ascetic who has conquered desire, smeared with ashes and haunting the cremation grounds. But at the

RIGHT *Shiva the cosmic dancer; he dances the endless rhythms of creation and destruction. The significance of Shiva's dance becomes clearer if one remembers that a dance is at once a free expression of the will and an action directed by exterior laws – if you like, by the rhythm of the music of time. Thus Shiva is a god, but he is defined by larger ineffable patterns.*

same time he is erotic, the great lover and passionate husband.

To the philosopher these opposing qualities are a paradox, but to the worshipper they represent the richness of existence and the totality of the divine being. The ultimate reconciliation of the conflicts embodied by Shiva is brought about when half his body becomes female and half of him remains male. There are many stories about Shiva and his exploits. In this one he safeguards immortality:

LEFT *The Divine Couple, Shiva and Parvati, with their children at the burning-ground; behind them is Shiva's mount, the bull Nandi. Shiva's son, the elephant-headed Ganesh, helps him to make a necklace of skulls. Parvati holds the six-headed son Karttikeya; (18th-century).*

BELOW LEFT *Hindu temple sculpture of Shiva and Parvati as one, half male, half female figure.*

SHIVA'S BLUE THROAT

BELOW *Shiva Nataraja, Lord of the Dance (10th-century Chola bronze from Madras state, southern India); one of the most famous of all Hindu icons, still reproduced to this day. The legend associated with this image involves the subjugation of ten thousand heretical holymen. They sent a tiger against him but Shiva flayed it and took its skin as a cape. A poisonous snake attacked him and he just hung it round his neck as a garland. Next a black dwarf attacked him with a club, but Shiva put one foot on him and danced until the dwarf and the holymen acknowledged him as the supreme master. The drum he holds in his upper right hand beats out the rhythm of creation. The single flame in his upper left hand is the flame of*

Following the advice of Vishnu, the gods and the demons were churning the celestial ocean of milk to obtain from it the nectar of immortality. For a churning rope they used the divine serpent Vasuki, and the great mountain Mandara was the churning rod. They churned furiously for 100 years. Among the first gifts of the celestial ocean were the beautiful goddess Lakshmi, who rose from a lotus flower floating on the rippling waves, and the divine cow Surabhi whose son Nandi, the snow-white bull, later became Shiva's companion and mount. The next gift was a crescent moon which Shiva snatched from the waves and placed on his forehead. Suddenly a terrible poisonous venom began gushing from the serpent's 1,000 mouths, threatening all existence. Moved by the request of the great Vishnu, Shiva swallowed the poison as if it were the nectar of immortality, thereby saving existence from extermination. The serpent's poison was harmless to the great Shiva but the venom stained his throat dark blue.

In painting Shiva is frequently portrayed with a blue throat and has acquired the epithet Nilakantha, or Blue Throat. A popular image of Shiva is that of Lord of the Dance, and he is frequently surrounded by a ring of sacred fire. This icon represents his five divine functions: creation, preservation, destruction, revelation (of the concealment of ignorance), and release (from rebirth).

But Shiva is most often worshipped as the *lingam*. The *lingam* is usually a cylinder of dark, shiny stone with a curved top set in a circular receptacle, or *yoni*, the symbol of female sexuality. Sometimes there are carvings of the five heads of Shiva on the *lingam*. It represents not only sexuality and the male creative force, but also chastity, as the seed is contained and controlled by yogic meditations. Mythology thrives on such paradoxes and there are many stories of the conflicts and

destruction. His lower right hand is held in a gesture of benediction to his devotees. This is reaffirmed by his lower left hand which is drooping in imitation of an elephant's trunk and pointing towards his upraised left foot, a symbolic gesture promising release from Samsara, or rebirth, to his followers. His right foot crushes the demon of ignorance symbolized by the dwarf. The ring of sacred fire represents both the cosmos itself and also the final release from Samsara, by its association with the cremation ground.

ABOVE *Stone Shiva icon in the form of a Lingam symbolizing divine power. The face carved on it represents the indwelling deity. A lingam occupies a sacred spot in all temples dedicated to Shiva (7th–8th century, Kashmir).*

struggles of Shiva as the erotic ascetic and of the problems of his unconventional married life. This tale tells of the rivalry between Shiva and Daksha, the father of his wife Sati. It is with reference to this story that the name Sati is given to the horrendous practice of throwing a widow on her husband's funeral pyre, imbuing what is an act of social and economic expediency with a ritual significance.

THE DEATH OF SATI

Daksha was holding a grand sacrifice to which all the gods were invited except Shiva. Sati was furious and decided to go since it was her own father's house. Shiva was pleased at

Ithyphallic figure of Shiva in his creative aspect; it is the double nature of Hindu gods that sometimes puzzles western observers (it is this confounding of opposites, this apparent lack of moral or metaphysical polarities, that destroys Mrs Moore in E. M. Forster's novel A Passage to India.

ABOVE *Shiva walking with the bull Nandi, followed by his consort Parvati; (c. 1730–40 painting from Mandi, north-west India).*

RIGHT *Stone icon of Shiva and Parvati.*

her loyalty and fervour but he warned her to be strong. 'Daksha will insult me and if you are unable to tolerate his insults, I fear you may come to harm,' he said. Sati arrived at the sacrifice and told her father, 'My lord is deep in meditation, I come alone.' Daksha laughed, seeing his chance to heap insults on his great rival. 'It is a disgrace for a god to wear filthy rags, to adorn himself with snakes and dance like a madman. I could never understand how a daughter of mine could wish for a creature like that for a husband.'

Sati, trembling with rage, denounced her father before the assembled gods. Since Shiva had instructed her not to take revenge she immolated herself on the sacrificial

The extremely popular elephant-headed god Ganesh, also known as 'The Remover of Obstacles'. His nature is gentle and affectionate and his image is found installed over the main entrance of many Indian homes to ward off evil. Symbolically, his round fat body contains the whole universe, his bended trunk can remove obstacles and his four arms represent the categories that the world can be divided into (that is the four castes). The sculpture is from Uttar Pradesh, c. 750 AD.

fire. Shiva's rage and torment at the loss of his beloved wife created a fearful demon who destroyed everyone who had been at the ceremony. Only when Vishnu interceded did Shiva relent and bring them all back to life. Daksha finally acknowledged that Shiva was a greater god than he, and as a sign of his foolishness he wore the head of a goat. Shiva fell into a profound meditation, waiting for the time when his beloved would be reincarnated as Parvati and be his wife again.

One of the children of Shiva and Parvati is Ganesh, the elephant-headed god. He is the general of Shiva's army, the patron of learning, the giver of good fortune and a popular deity today. At the beginning of books he is invoked by poets, his image is placed on the ground when a new house is built and he is honoured before a journey is begun or any business undertaken. This is the story of how he came to have an elephant's head:

THE ELEPHANT-HEADED GOD

Shiva had been away for years and Parvati was bored and lonely. She decided to make herself a baby to play with and fashioned a small roly-poly boy out of clay. One day when Parvati was bathing in a pool she asked her

RIGHT *The goddess
Durga killing the
buffalo demon
Mahisha. In her eight
arms she carries
weapons lent to her by
the gods; (13th-century
stone sculpture from
Orissa).*

son Ganesh to make sure no one disturbed her. Shiva arrived home at that moment and started to look for Parvati. The boy, not realizing who it was, stopped him from going near the pool. Furious at being opposed, Shiva immediately cut off the boy's head with his sword. Parvati's grief knew no bounds, she screamed and threw herself sobbing on the ground. To placate her, Shiva sent 1,000 goblins, demons and imps to look for the head of a male child. They searched all night but finding each baby animal asleep facing his mother they did not have the heart to cut off his head. Finally they found a baby elephant who was sleeping with his head turned away from his mother so his trunk didn't get entangled with his mother's and prevent them snuggling close together. Immediately Shiva's goblins removed his head and brought it to him. As he fitted the elephant's head onto his child's body he breathed life into it and waited for Parvati's reaction. To his surprise, she was delighted.

Shiva's bride is a perfect wife in the forms of Sati and Parvati, but like Shiva, she also has her horrible forms. As Durga she is the beautiful and ferocious warrior goddess, and as the hideous personification of death and destruction she is Kali, the black earth mother. As Kali, she is usually depicted naked save for a girdle of giant's heads suspended from her waist. She has long, flowing hair and a long necklace of giant's skulls around her neck. Like Shiva, she has a flaming third eye on her forehead. She is usually depicted with four arms: in one she holds a weapon, and in another the dripping head of a giant; two empty hands are raised to bless her worshippers. She is covered by a tiger skin and her long tongue protrudes, thirsty for blood. To her devotees, Kali is a divine and loving mother who reveals to them the reality of mortality. She not only destroys demons but also death itself. She appeals especially to those who find the mother–child relationship and

RIGHT Kali, the mother goddess in her horrible form; (9th-century stone icon from Orissa). She is holding a sword and wearing a garland of skulls.

symbol more satisfying as a revelation of the divine reality:

KALI'S DANCE OF DEATH

A wicked monster was ravaging the world. He seemed invincible because every drop of blood that he spilled came to life and became 1,000 more demons ready to battle. The gods summoned Kali and asked her to destroy the monster. Leaping into battle, the terrible goddess slayed 1,000 demons with her whirling sword. As she killed them she drank their blood,

licking up the drops before they could touch the ground and produce more demons. Finally only the original monster was left and she consumed him in one gulp. Beginning her victory dance she became more and more frenzied and out of control, threatening all creation. Fearing that the universe would be destroyed, the gods came to her husband Shiva and begged him to intercede and stop her wild dance of destruction. But she paid no heed even to him, until in desperation he threw himself down before her. She began to dance on his body. Eventually, realizing what she was doing, she came out of her trance and stopped dancing. Thus the universe was saved from the ravages of the mad dance of Kali.

Vishnu is the most widely worshipped of the Hindu gods. He is all-

ABOVE *Vishnu in his 10th and future incarnation as the white horse Kalkin; (c. 1780 miniature from Bilaspur, Madhya Pradesh).*

LEFT *Vishnu worshipped in five manifestations; an illustration from the Hindu text* Vishnu Samabranahama. *(17th- century painting).*

pervading, the preserver of the world, and his function is to ensure the triumph of good against evil. To this end he comes to earth on many occasions in different incarnations. The most famous are his lives as the epic heroes Krishna and Rama, but there are also the fish, the tortoise, the boar, the man-lion, the dwarf, Parashurama, Buddha and Kalkin.

These incarnations show how Hinduism has taken over and absorbed popular folk deities and the tales associated with them. Vishnu is often depicted with four arms. He holds in his hands the characteristic symbols of the wheel (the powers of creation and destruction), the conch shell (associated with the origin of existence through its spiral form, its sound, and its connection with water), and the club (authority or the power of know-ledge), and his fourth hand has an up-raised palm expressing reassurance.

Vishnu's consort in all his incarnations is Lakshmi, the popular goddess of wealth and good fortune. She is also known as the fickle one as she is a wanderer who never stays long with anyone. During the festival of Diwali in the late autumn, thousands of tiny lanterns are lit all over India, houses are cleaned and decorated until they too are sparkling, and fireworks are let off. All this is to please Lakshmi who is wandering from house to house looking for somewhere to spend the night and blessing with prosperity all those houses that are well lit.

In his incarnation as a fish, Matsya, Vishnu saved Manu from a great flood so that his descendants could people the world:

RIGHT *Vishnu in his Lion incarnation.*

FAR RIGHT *Vishnu in his Boar incarnation, lifting the earth-goddess Bhumi from the primeval ocean; (12th-century Chaunan-style stone icon from Punjab).*

VISHNU
THE PRESERVER

While bathing in the river one day, Manu found a tiny fish. The fish begged him to rescue him from the other big fish who wanted to eat him. Manu scooped up the little fish and took him home in an earthenware pot. but Matsya, the fish, soon grew too big for the pot and Manu dug a pond for him to live in. When Matsya had grown too big for the pond he asked Manu to take him to the ocean and release him. As Manu tossed Matsya into the ocean, the fish turned and spoke to him. He warned Manu that in a year's time there would be a great flood, and told him to build a ship to save himself as the whole world would be submerged. Manu did as Matsya had told him and when the flood came he took refuge in his ship, praising Matsya for saving him. As the storms grew fierce and dangerous, Matsya appeared again. Now an enormous fish with golden scales and a horn, he attached the ship's cable to his horn and towed it along. Pulling the ship behind him, Matsya swam for many years until they reached mount Hemavat, the top of which was still above the water. Manu moored the ship to the mountain to await the end of the flood. Before he left, Matsya announced that he was really Vishnu the Preserver and had saved Manu from the flood in order that he might create new plants, animals and people for the world.

Krishna is the most beloved of all the Hindu gods. For his worshippers he embodies divine beauty, joy, and love. The playfulness of the divine child and the charming and tender love of the divine youth draw the devotees into the loving embrace of the supreme God. This is the story of the life of Krishna:

BELOW *Vishnu in his fish incarnation, Matsya.*

THE YOUNG
KRISHNA

The gods wanted someone to destroy the evil king Kans of Mathura, so Vishnu resolved to be born as the eighth son of the king's sister Devaki. King Kans was warned of this scheme and he imprisoned Devaki and her husband Vasudev and killed each of their sons as they were born. But when Krishna was born Vishnu appeared to the couple and told them to exchange their baby son for the newborn daughter of a cowherd couple, Yasodha and Nanda, who lived in the village of Gokul across the river Yamuna. Vasudev found the doors of the prison miraculously open and set

ABOVE *Radha and Krishna in the Grove; (18th-century Pahari painting from the hill state of Kangra in Punjab). All nature rejoices in the couple's bliss and their embrace is echoed by the vine which encircles the tree in the foreground.*

off for Gokul with the child. He had to cross the river Yamuna in a terrible storm and feared for their safety. The baby Krishna touched the water with his foot and the waves parted, letting them through. Vasudev left the baby with Yasodha, who brought him up as her own son, and returned to jail with the baby girl who was no threat to King Kans. However, the king found out that Krishna had been saved and sent a demon nurse called Patoona to destroy him. The demon managed to deceive Yasodha and Nanda, but when she gave her breast to the baby Krishna he sucked and sucked until he had sucked all of Patoona's life away. As a child Krishna was playful and mischievous. Innocent and obedient in his mother's presence, he missed no opportunity for mischief when her back was turned. He untied the village calves and pulled their tails, mocked and laughed at his elders and teased

73

RIGHT *The young Krishna striking the cow with his cowherd's flask; his half-brother Balaram stands behind. The scene takes place beneath a Bo-tree; (10th-century stone relief carving).*

BELOW *Krishna subdues the snake demon by dancing on its head; (19th-century fragment of a temple painting from Madras).*

little babies until they cried, urinated in neighbours' houses and stole butter and sweets. But Yasodha and Nanda, who have no control over him, just laughed at his antics. When Krishna was about 12 he slew Kaliya, the five-headed serpent king who had been killing chickens, goats and cattle. He also destroyed the demon Trinavarta who was sent by King Kans disguised as a whirlwind. As a youth, Krishna enchanted and intoxicated the cowherd women with his flute playing. He teased them and made love to them. His favourite was the beautiful Radha, who took many risks to meet her dark lover:

How can I describe his relentless
  flute,
which pulls virtuous women from
  their homes
and drags them by their hair to
  Krishna
as thirst and hunger pull the doe to
  the snare?

Chaste ladies forget their lords,
wise men forget their wisdom,
and clinging vines shake loose from
  their trees,
hearing that music.

(David R. Kinsley, *The Sword and the Flute*).

BELOW *Gopis (cowherds) begging Krishna to return their clothes. He has stolen them while the Gopis are bathing to tease them; (18th-century Kangra painting).*

Eventually, stories of Krishna's exploits reached King Kans and he resolved to try and kill him again.

THE WRESTLING CONTEST

The king announced a wrestling match and challenged the local young men to try and beat the court champions. His plan was to lure Krishna and his brother Balaram into the city and, pretending that it was an accident, release a wild elephant in their path. He felt sure that they would not survive such an encounter. Krishna and Balaram seized the chance to show off their prowess at wrestling and came to the city on the day of the festivities. When their turn came, they entered the ring to be faced by a wild elephant charging towards them

BELOW *A highly stylized 18th-century portrait of Radha from Kishangarh in Rajasthan. The painter Nihal Chand is thought to have derived this style from the poetry of his patron, Raja Savant Singh, describing his own beloved whose nose was 'curved and sharp like the thrusting saru cypress plant'.*

RIGHT *Rama with his bow; (16th-century bronze from Madras).*

trumpeting in fury. Without hesitating, Krishna leapt upon the elephant, and putting his mighty arms around its neck he squeezed until the creature fell beneath him dead. The crowd cheered and King Kans, more furious and frightened than ever, sent his fearsome champions into the ring. But they were no match for the brothers. Krishna soon broke the neck of the first, and Balaram squeezed the second in a great bear hug until his heart burst. Then Krishna leapt upon King Kans and flung him against the wall, killing him in front of the assembled crowds. He then freed his parents and his grandfather, who was the rightful king.

Many more exploits and marriages of Krishna are recounted in the epic poem, the *Mahabharata*. It is into his mouth that tradition puts the *Bhagavad Gita*, one of the most sacred books of modern Hinduism.

Rama is the hero of the other great epic, the *Ramayana*, and another incarnation of Vishnu, sent to earth to kill the demon Ravana. His wife, Sita, is considered to be the perfect wife and her behaviour is held up to young girls to emulate. Sita was abducted by

BELOW *A 20th-century depiction of Hanuman, the monkey god, causing mischief among people; note the flames he carries (top right). In the story related (right), Hanuman is protected by Agni, the god of fire.*

the demon Ravana and carried off to his Kingdom of Lanka and the distraught Rama went in search of her. In the forest he enlisted the help of the monkey god Hanuman. In this extract Hanuman uses his magic powers to reach Lanka and discovers Sita:

HANUMAN THE MONKEY GOD

Hanuman learned from Sampati, the brother of the king of the vultures, that Sita had been carried off to the distant island of Lanka, a hundred leagues over the southern ocean. Being the son of Vayu, the wind god, Hanuman resolved to use his powers to leap over the sea. He filled his lungs with sea wind and, with a mighty roar, rushed to the top of a mountain. Assuming a gigantic form, he leapt into the air and sped across the sea like an arrow. But his path through the air was impeded by demons. Surasa opened her enormous jaws to catch him, but he quickly shrunk to the size of a man's thumb and leapt in and out of her gaping mouth before she could close it. Next his shadow was grabbed by the she-dragon Sinhika who wanted to devour him. But he wounded and killed her and carried on to the island. Arriving at night he turned himself into a cat and crept stealthily around the sumptuous palace looking for Sita. Creeping up the jewelled stairways of gold and silver he came across the women's chamber. The perfumed forms asleep seemed like a wreath of lotus blooms awaiting the kiss of the morning sun. Outside, in a grove of Asoka trees, Hanuman saw the long-lost Sita. Guarded by fierce and ugly demons with the heads of dogs and pigs, she was without fear. Although Ravana came daily, threatening her with torture and death if she would not marry him, she rejected him. She would die before she was unfaithful to Rama.

LEFT *Hanuman, the monkey god, from a Vaishnavite shrine; (11th-century Tamilwork bronze from Sri Lanka).*

Hanuman secretly approached the beautiful, sorrowing Sita and showed her Rama's ring that he was carrying. He offered to carry her away, but her modesty prevented her from touching the body of any man except her husband. Instead she gave him a jewel from her hair and begged him to tell Rama that she had only two months to live if he did not rescue her. Before he left, Hanuman decided to destroy as much of Ravana's kingdom as he could. Turning himself back into a giant monkey he started to uproot trees and devastate the countryside, but he was taken prisoner by Ravana's son, the mighty Indrajit, who shot him with a magic serpent arrow. As a gesture of defiance, Ravana set Hanuman's tail on fire and sent him back to Rama as an envoy. But Sita prayed that he would not burn and Agni, the god of fire, spared him. As he escaped from the kingdom of Lanka, Hanuman managed to accomplish great destruction by setting fire to many mansions with his flaming tail. When he returned, Rama was overjoyed that his beloved Sita had been found and immediately made preparations to go to her rescue.

SPIRIT OF THE BUDDHA

Buddhism originated in India but spread to the countries of south-east Asia where it has become a major religious and cultural force. Buddhist thought shares with Hinduism its cosmological vision of time, including the transmigration of souls. Gautama Buddha was born in northern India in the 6th century BC. But the story of his life has become a legend which illustrates the main precepts of Buddhist thought.

The spirit of the Buddha appeared to Queen Maya of Kapilavastu in a dream: an elephant floating on a raincloud, a symbol of fertility, circled around her three times and then entered her womb. Astrologers forecast that Queen Maya and King Suddhodana would have a son who would leave the palace to become a holy man. When the baby was born, a lotus sprang from the place where he first touched the ground. Fearing that Prince Siddhartha would leave as had been prophesied, the King surrounded him with luxury. At 16 he was married to the princess Yasodhara, and 12 years later their only child Rahula was born. At about this time Siddhartha's curiosity about the outside world was aroused and he ventured outside the palace grounds. Outside, he encountered for the first time old age, sick-

LEFT *Seated Buddha in Dharmachakra attitude; (c. 1st century AD Gandhara style sculpture from Yusufzai).*

RIGHT *Gautama Buddha 'The presentation of bowls'; (relief from Buner c. 2nd–3rd century AD Gandhara). A Buddhist monk's begging bowl is a concrete manifestation of his vow of poverty.*

ness and death and was awakened to suffering. He also met a wandering ascetic and resolved to leave his home and become a recluse. After six years of extreme asceticism he realized that he was no nearer enlightenment than he had been while living in luxury, and he resolved to follow a middle way to enlightenment, free from desire. While meditating, Siddhartha was tested by the demon Mara, first with fear and then with pleasure, but he was untouched. Eventually, he achieved insight into all his former existences. He became aware of how the terrible suffering that wastes human life is caused and how it can be eliminated, recognizing the four noble truths that became the basis of his teaching: that suffering exists; that it depends on certain conditions; that these conditions can be removed; and that the way to remove these conditions is to practise the eight-fold path – right views, right resolve, right speech, right conduct, right liveli-

BELOW *The 'Sanci torso'; red sandstone torso of a Bodhisattva from Sanci (Gupta period, 5th–9th century).*

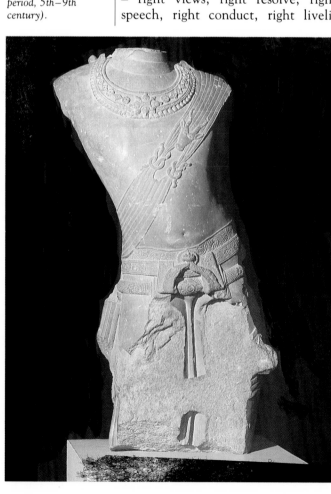

hood, right effort, right mindfulness, and right concentration. Forty-nine days later he set in motion the 'wheel of teaching' by preaching his first sermon in the deer park at Sarnath. His deep sense of compassion induced him to preach for the next 45 years.

The Jataka tales are a collection of 550 stories of the former lives of the Buddha. Some of these tales are peculiarly Buddhistic, but others are evidently part of the contemporary folk lore and have been incorporated into Buddhist mythology. They give us a vivid picture of the social life and customs of ancient India. Some of these tales are quite misogynistic; women are often viewed as the source of all treachery, as in this story about a demon – or *asura* – who used to come and listen to the preaching of the Boddhisattva. The story is a moral tale which warns against hankering after worldly pleasures, although an alternative interpretation might be that it is about the wiliness of women:

'WELCOME ALL THREE OF YOU'

The *asura* lived in the forest next to the highway. When he was not catching and devouring unwary travellers, the *asura* would go and listen to the teaching of the Boddhisattva. One day, he devoured the bodyguard of an exceedingly beautiful noblewoman of the area. She was so beautiful that he carried her off to his cave and took her for his wife. He brought her good things to eat, clarified butter, husked rice, fish, flesh and fresh fruit. He dressed her in rich robes and ornaments. And to keep her safe he put her in a box which he swallowed, thus guarding her in his belly.

One day, the *asura* went to the river to bathe. He threw up the box and let her out to enjoy herself in the open air while he bathed a little way off. While the *asura* was away she saw

BELOW *Stone relief representation of the great stupa at Amaravati (now destroyed) from its own casing; (Andhra Pradesh c. 150–200 AD). Buddhist stupas developed form burial mounds containing relics of the Buddha to vast representations of the cosmos and centres of Buddhist worship during the period of the Mauryan dynasty (c. 322–185 BC), when Buddhism was the imperial religion. The stupa was exported with Buddhism and in China evolved into the tiered tower pagoda.*

LEFT *Stone relief illustrating the Vassantara Jataka tale; in this story of one of the Buddha's previous incarnations he was prince Vessantara, seen here giving his chariot to a Brahmin beggar.*

OVERLEAF LEFT *Stone relief depicting worshippers circumambulating a stupa; this ritual was performed by entering the east gate and walking clockwise, symbolically following the course of the sun and putting the worshipper in touch with the cosmos and the spiritual world.*

OVERLEAF RIGHT *Sections of a frieze showing the birth of the Buddha; in the centre is Queen Maya, clutching the tree above her. On the right of the picture are her aristocratic female attendants. Catching the sacred baby is the god Indra and next to him is Brahma; (Schist relief, Gandhara style, 2nd century AD).*

a magician flying through the air and beckoned him to her. When the magician came to her she put him into the box, covering him with her own body and wrapping her garments around him. The Asura returned and swallowed the box again, not thinking there was anyone but the woman inside it.

He decided to go and listen to the teaching of the Boddhisattva again, and as he approached, the holy man greeted him saying, 'welcome all three of you'. The *asura* was curious to know what this meant as he had come alone to visit the ascetic, and the ascetic told him that he was carrying inside his belly not only his wife but also a magician. Fearing that the magician might rip open his belly to make his escape, the *asura* threw up the box again and found his wife and the magician in the box, sporting merrily. The demon was so amazed at the Boddhisattva's vision – and so thankful that his life had been saved from the sword of the magician – that he let the woman go and praised the wisdom of the holy man:

O stern ascetic, thy clear vision saw
How low poor man, a woman's slave
    may sink;
As life itself tho' guarded in my maw,
The wretch did play the wanton, as I
    think.

I tended her with care both day and
night,
As forest hermit cherishes a flame,
And yet she sinned, beyond all sense
of right:
To do with woman needs must end in
shame.

(Jataka: *Stories of Buddha's Former
Births*, Ed. E. B. Cowell)

In other Jataka tales the Buddha is
born as an animal. In one he is a
monkey who lived alone on the river
bank. It is comparable to an Aesop's
fable where cleverness outwits force.
In Indian tales it is often the crocodile
or the tiger, the dangerous animals,
who are depicted as fools.

THE FOUR
VIRTUES

In the middle of the river was an
island on which grew many fruit
trees bearing mangoes, bread-fruit
and other good things to eat. Each
day the monkey would go to the island by jumping first onto a large rock
that stuck out of the water, using it as
a stepping stone to the island. He
would eat his fill and then return home
every evening by the same route.
Now, there was a crocodile living in
the river who was searching for food
for his pregnant wife. He determined
to catch the monkey by lying in wait
for him on the rock. On his way home
the monkey noticed that the rock was
rather higher in the river than usual
and called out 'Hi rock!' three times.
There was silence, so the wise monkey
called out, 'Why don't you speak to
me today, friend?' The foolish crocodile, thinking that the monkey was
really expecting the rock to answer
shouted out, 'It's me, the crocodile,
waiting to catch you and eat your
heart'. The crafty monkey agreed to
give himself up and told the crocodile
to open his mouth to catch him when
he jumped. As is well known, when

crocodiles open their mouths their
eyes close. So while the crocodile
could not see him the monkey used
him as his stepping stone, leaping
onto his back and then onto the bank
of the river and home. The crocodile
realized how clever the monkey had
been and said, 'Monkey, he that in
this world possesses the four virtues
overcomes his foes. And you, I think,
possess all four'. (The four virtues are
friendliness, compassion, joy and
equanimity.) Tales like these provide
endless subject matter for the sculptor
and painter, particularly as no images
of the Buddha were made at first and
he was only symbolized by a wheel,
his sandals, his stool or a Bodi-tree.
The railings of the great Buddhist
stupas at Barhut and Sanchi are teem-
ing with the characters from these
familiar tales, each one with a moral.

Muslims entered India as early as
the year 711, by the same north-
western route as the ancient Aryan
conquerors. In the 17th century the
Mughal empire, famous for its glitter-
ing court, ruled almost all of the Indian
subcontinent. Islam and Hinduism
are two very different traditions and
Islamic philosophy did not flourish as
much on Indian soil as elsewhere.
The literature of the Muslim community came more from Persian traditions. But the meeting of the two
cultures did bear fruit. There were
areas of common ground in discussion
of monism and monotheism, in the
traditions of saints, and especially in
the mystic and devotional movements
of both religions. Examples of a literature that is both Indian and Muslim
are the medieval tales of romantic
love. This 'Enchanting Story' is from
the 18th-century poet Mir Hasan:

PRINCESS
BADR I MUNIR

The beautiful young prince Benazir
was captured by a fairy named
Marhukh. She allowed him out on a

magic carpet each evening on condition that if he lost his heart to another he would tell her. One night on his travels he came across a group of young women by a watercourse. In the centre of the group was the 15-year-old Princess Badr i Munir, clothed in fine and delicate fabrics and adorned with pearls and other priceless jewels. When their eyes met they were both smitten with love and fell down in a swoon. Their affair developed, assisted by Badr i Munir's closest friend Najm un Nisa, until the fairy discovered it. Furious at being deceived, she imprisoned Benazir at the bottom of a dried-up well in the middle of the desert, guarded by a jinn. When Benazir came no more to their rendezvous, Badr i Munir grew sick with love and sorrow and disappointment. She lost her appetite and wandered about distracted. Crying herself to sleep one night she dreamt of Benazir and saw his plight. Her friend Najm un Nisa decided to go in search of him. Dis-

BELOW *An Indian marriage; a painting of the Mughal school from Lucknow, 1775.*

LEFT *Eighteenth-century painting from Guler (Chandigarh Museum); in front of the pavilion where the prince and his wife lay is a pool with lotus flowers, while on the roof is a peacock, a symbol of the lover. A pair of love birds are in the trees in the foreground.*

guised as an ascetic and carrying a lute, she set off. The beauty of her playing attracted the attention of Firoz Shah, the handsome son of the king of the jinns. Her own beauty shone through her disguise and captured his heart, so he carried her off to his father's palace. She stayed at court for some time, playing the lute each evening, until the prince was hopelessly in love with her and begged her to marry him. Before she would agree to his proposal she explained her mission to him and asked for his help in finding Benazir. The king of the jinns sent fairies to discover his whereabouts and rebuked Mahrukh for forming such an attachment to a human. Finally Benazir was released from his prison and brought to the palace. Firoz Shah had a magic, flying throne, and on it he carried Najm un Nisa and Benazir back to the garden of Badr i Munir. Their reunion was sweet. Their bodies weak from the sorrow of separation and their eyes red from weeping, they talked long into the night and slept late into the morning. The following day all four of them took all the necessary steps to ensure that they might be married. The weddings were celebrated with great

87

LEFT *Garland seller in Old Delhi; the number of festivals in India is so great that he is kept busy throughout the year. On the tenth day of the rising moon between September and October falls the most popular of Indian festivals – Dussehra – a celebration of a great victory by Rama over the Demon King Ravana. An estimated crowd of five million gathered at Uttar Pradesh for the Hindu festival of Kumbh-Mela in 1966, possibly the greatest number of human beings ever assembled with a common purpose.*

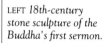

LEFT *18th-century stone sculpture of the Buddha's first sermon.*

pomp and ceremony, thus fulfilling the heart's desire of all four lovers.

Almost every day of the year somewhere in India a festival is held. At the most popular festivals thousands of people gather to listen to stories of their favourite heroes and gods. At the *Rama-lila,* held in Delhi in the autumn, there are theatrical performances of the great battle between Rama and Ravana, the demon king of Lanka, who kidnapped Rama's wife Sita. The performance ends with the immolation of a vast paper effigy of Ravana.

Most of the dates of the calender are marked by an event that celebrates the myths and traditions of the culture. In the villages of Maharashtra, in western India, when the new har-

vest of rice is gathered in, the villagers dance around a heap of grains with an image of a deity on top. They play a ritualistic riddle game, one half of the dancers asking the questions and the other half responding. In this way they build up a familiar story, usually out of one of the great epics. Although Indian mythology has very ancient roots, it punctuates the rhythms of everyday life and is very much alive today.

BELOW *A princess and her ladies celebrating Diwali, the festival of lights, in a palace garden, with yogis and yoginis; (a painting of the Mughal school by Hunhar, c. 1760).*

Japanese Mythology

In January 1989, Emperor Hirohito of Japan died. The enthronement ceremony of the new emperor, Akihito, was done according to Shinto tradition, for the emperor has always been the head of Japan's national religion. But opposition parties in the Japanese democracy strongly criticized the idea of employing Shinto rituals in the ceremonies concerning the funeral and the enthronement. State Shintoism is a relatively new phenomenon, started about one-and-a-half centuries ago in order to unify Japan after the long period of feudalism. It took only a few decades for this artificial state Shintoism to get out of control, and the Emperor's position as a human-god was abused, mostly by the army, to justify the invasion of neighbouring countries. It is from Shinto that the authentic Japanese mythology comes, particularly from the Kojiki, the 'Record of Ancient Things' (completed in the eighth century AD), which became a kind of statement of Shinto orthodoxy.

Paper screen by Ogata Korin (1658–1716) decorated with pink and white plum blossoms.

Traditional Shinto, as opposed to state Shintoism, has its origin about 2,000 years ago. Shinto is Japan's primal religion and is integrated into Japan's culture. Around the 3rd century BC, a Japan consisting of a single race and a single language emerged after a long period of racial and cultural diversity (though the political unification of Japan was not completed by the imperial family until the 6th century AD). Japan's birth as a nation coincided with the start of rice growing – Japan's main industry until quite

recently – and Shinto consisted of rituals to pray for a good harvest, keeping the community unified through those rituals. The fact that people were primarily considered as members of the community rather than as individuals explains Shinto's survival despite of the powerful influence of Buddhism: more than 70% of the Japanese were engaged in agriculture up to the end of the Second World War.

An agricultural life is hard work, and requires activity to be coordinated with the changing seasons. This inte-

ABOVE AND BELOW
Sections of a long scroll painting in black ink, 'Landscape for Four Seasons' by Sesshu, 1486.

LEFT *Float decorated in the time-honoured tradition for the annual Gion festival in Kyoto.*

ABOVE *Head of Haniwa, a grave figurine, from the 6th century AD.*

LEFT *Izumo shrine, Shimane prefecture, the oldest Shinto shrine in Japan; the Shinto gods are supposed to assemble here in October each year, thus October is termed the 'godless month' elsewhere.*

gration of people's beliefs with their working lives still exists in Japanese companies today – it is a common practice to build small Shinto shrines on top of the office buildings – but modern industrial work lacks the sensitivity to nature required for rice growing. Nature and the changing seasons were not seen as romantic or beautiful, but life was lived according to the dictates of the seasons. So not surprisingly, the concepts of virtue in Shintoism are reflected in the success, or failure, of farming. The notions of purity, or clarity, and uncleanliness, or filth, are the most fundamental concepts in Shintoism; the word *kegare* is Japanese for uncleanliness, and stems from *ke* meaning a mythical power to make things grow, and *gare* meaning lacking. Together, *kegare* therefore means a lack of power to make things grow (and particularly rice), and uncleanliness is thus associated with failure to thrive.

The main record of Shinto myth and historical legend is the *Kojiki*, the Record of Ancient Things, completed in 712 AD. Divided into three books, the first covering life with the gods, the second life with Man and the gods, and the third, Man's life without the gods. It also covers the origins of the imperial clan and the leading families. The *Kojiki* has until recently been regarded as sacred. Many of its stories involve these key concepts of purity and uncleanliness.

RIGHT *Rengyoin temple was founded in 1164 and rebuilt in 1266 after a fire. It contains 1001 small figurines of Kwannon, known in China as Guanyin, the Goddess of Mercy.*

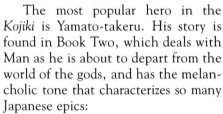

The most popular hero in the *Kojiki* is Yamato-takeru. His story is found in Book Two, which deals with Man as he is about to depart from the world of the gods, and has the melancholic tone that characterizes so many Japanese epics:

FRATRICIDE WITHOUT REMORSE

Among the many children of Emperor Keiko were the brothers Opo-usu and Wo-usu, the second of whom was later named Yamato-takeru. One day the emperor sent Opo-usu to summon two maidens who were renowned for their beauty. But instead of summoning them, Opo-usu made them his wives and sent others in their stead. When the emperor learned of his son's betrayal, he ordered Wo-usu to persuade his elder brother to come to dine with his father. Five days passed, but Opo-usu still did not come. When the emperor asked Wo-usu why his brother had not come, Wo-usu explained 'I captured him, grasped him, and crushed him, then pulled off his limbs, and wrapping them in a straw mat, I threw them away'.

This example of brute strength without any regard to morality explains why Yamato-takeru is seen as an embodiment of natural force, beyond the understanding of a mortal being. Nature brings about harvest, and at

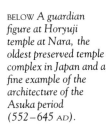

BELOW *A guardian
figure at Horyuji
temple at Nara, the
oldest preserved temple
complex in Japan and a
fine example of the
architecture of the
Asuka period
(552–645 AD).*

the same time can be utterly destructive. It is to be admired and feared.

Throughout, the style of the *Kojiki* is realistic, and often cruelly bloody. This violence is in evidence throughout the adventures of Yamato-takeru as he is sent by his father the emperor to quell both real political enemies, and also 'unruly' deities. Japan's natural sport, Sumo, is characterized by its display of sheer power. Wrestlers are often very quiet people and are expected to live simply. We can see in Sumo the same sort of admiration as that shown for the boy-hero Yamato-takeru. There are many elements of Shinto ritual in Sumo. Wrestlers throw salt before each bout to purify the ring. They use water put beside the ring to clean their mouths, symbolizing the purification of the bodies. The ring is made of packed soil inside which there are various things dedicated to gods.

CLEANSING
BY FIRE

Yamato-takeru next embarked on a long journey as the emperor dispatched him to destroy rebel forces.

First he was sent to the west to kill
two mighty brothers; when he arrived
at their house he found it surrounded
by rows of warriors. Yamato-takeru
was so young (perhaps 15 or 16) that
he could disguise himself as a young
girl by combing his hair down and
dressing in women's clothes. He went
into the house while the feast was
taking place. The brothers were very
pleased to see this 'girl' and had her
sit between them. Then, when the
feast was at its height, Yamato-takeru
seized one of the brothers by the collar
and stabbed him clear through the
chest. The younger brother ran, but
Yamato-takeru seized him and stabbed
him too.

On his return home, Yamato-takeru
subdued and pacified all the mountain,
river and sea deities, but it was not
long before the emperor commanded

LEFT *Splashed-ink
landscape by Sesshu,
given by the artist to
his pupil. The
accompanying text
explains how he went
to China to learn this
particular technique.
The influence of China
upon Japanese art and
Japanese mythology is
widespread.*

ABOVE *Print by Utamaro (1754–1806) of young women visiting the seashore at Ise; at New Year the sun rises between the twin rocks, joined by a straw rope that marks the boundary of the territory of the gods.*

Yamato-takeru to deal with more unrest in the east. Yamato-takeru went to his aunt Yamato-pime, complaining that he was being sent out again too soon, and without adequate protection. On his departure, Yamato-pime gave him a sword, and a bag, and said 'Should there be an emergency, open this bag'.

Yamato-takeru, after conquering his father's enemies, met a man in the land of Sagamu who deceived him, saying that an unruly deity resided in the middle of the plain. When Yamato-takeru entered the plain, the man set fire to the area, but Yamato-takeru escaped using his aunt's bag and sword. He mowed the grass with his sword, then lit a counter-fire with a flint which he found in his aunt's bag. Then he killed the man and all his clan, burning the bodies.

One of the imperial treasures that Japan's new emperor Akihito inherited from the late Hirohito is a sword. A sword is one of the symbols of the figurehead of Shintoism, because it symbolizes lightning: thunder is re-

RIGHT *The traditional dance theatre, Kabuku, which is played by men only, has been popular since the 17th century.*

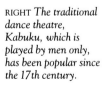

98

BELOW *Woodcut print by Hokusai of Tago-no-ura, in the series 'Thirty-six Views of Mount Fuji'.*

garded as promoting good harvest. The amount of thunder, and consequently rain, has most to do with the growth of rice. The idea of the gift of fire is so widespread that it would seem to be practically a part of racial memory: consider the Prometheus myth.

DEATH OF YAMATO-TAKERU

As Yamato-takeru crossed the sea, the deity of the crossing stirred up the waves, and the boat began to drift helplessly. His wife, Oto-tatiban-pime, offered to sacrifice herself to the sea god in his place, and stepped out onto layers of sedge-mats, skins and silk carpet spread out on the waves. As she went down onto them, she sang:

O you, my lord, alas –
You who once, standing among the
    flames
Of the burning fire, spoke my name
On the mountain-surrounded
Plain of Sagamu!

Seven days later, her comb was washed ashore. Taking this comb, they made

OVERLEAF *Waves at Matsushima by Tawaraya Sotatsu (1575–1643); ink, colour and gold on paper, Edo period.*

her tomb and place her within.

Yamato-takeru then experienced the first of the incidents that lead to his downfall. On his way back to the capital, when he was eating his rations at the foot of the pass of Asi-gara, the deity of the pass, assuming the form of a white deer, came and stood next to him. Yamato-takeru struck the deer with the leftovers from his meal, hitting the deer's eye and killing him. Then he climbed up the pass and, grieving, sighed three times: 'My wife, alas!'.

He is defeated by the deity of Mount Ibuki who causes a violent hail storm which dazes Yamato-takeru. His mind recovers a little as he rests at a spring, but because of his extreme fatigue he walks along slowly, using a staff. He proceeds across the plain of Tagi to the plain of Nobo, where he

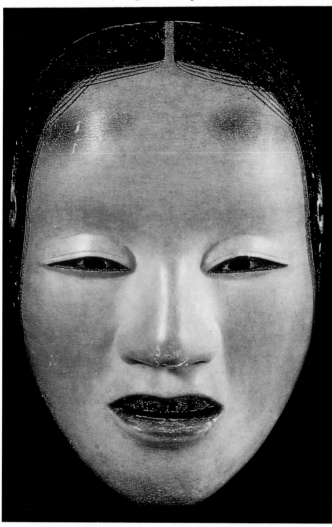

BELOW *Noh mask worn by an actor playing a middle-aged woman in the 15th-century drama Fukei by Tokuwaka.*

sings this song recalling his homeland:

> From the direction
> Of my beloved home
> The clouds are rising
> Next to the maiden's
> Sleeping place
> I left
> The sabre, the sword –
> Alas, that sword!

He dies. When his family come down to the plain of Nobo to construct his tomb, they also sing:

> The vines of the Tokoro
> Climb around
> Among the rice stems,
> The rice stems in the rice paddies
> Bordering the tomb.

The *Kojiki* has many beautiful songs such as these which anticipate *waka*, or *haiku*, Japanese poetical forms. They are symbolic rather than descriptive, their simplicity attempting to capture emotion or instantaneous thought without using words of emotion. The above song is meant to capture the desolate feeling of people who have lost the man they loved.

EXCLUDED FROM THE DIVINE

Transformed into a giant white bird, Yamato-takeru flew away toward the beach followed by his family:

> Moving with difficulty, up to our
>   waists
> In the field of low bamboo stalks,
> We cannot go through the skies
> but, alas, must go by foot.

As they waded into the sea, they sang:

> Going by sea, waist-deep in the
>   water
> We move forward with difficulty
> Like plants growing
> By a large river
> We drift aimlessly
> In the ocean currents.

ABOVE *The puppets in Bunraku theatre are manipulated by three people, clearly visible behind a narrow stage.*

Again, when the bird had flown to the rocky shores, they sang:

> The plover of the beach
> Does not go by the beaches
> But follows along the rocky shores

These concluding songs to the story of Yamato-takeru express the destiny of earth-bound man. The exclusion of

Man from the realm of the divine, and his struggle to return, is common to many mythologies from around the world. Some authorities believe that in this tale the flight of the bird is connected to the tradition of mourners dressing as birds to sing and dance at funerals. It is either an attempt to call back the soul that has flown away, or to assist the soul in its ascent to the higher regions.

Whereas the story of Yamato-takeru deals with the story of Man, Book One of the *Kojiki* concerns itself with the creation. The cosmology of the *Kojiki* is a step-by-step evolution of the universe. There is no creation from absolute nothing by an absolute being, and the creation of the islands of Japan is described thus:

THE BIRTH OF JAPAN

Two gods, Izanagi and Izanami, were given the command to create the islands, which they did by standing on the heavenly Floating Bridge and, lowering the heavenly Jewelled Spear, stirring with it. They stirred the brine

LEFT *The Jidai festival in Kyoto includes a 2½-mile-long procession of groups dressed in costumes representing styles from the late 8th to 19th centuries, celebrating Kyoto's time as the capital.*

ABOVE *When praying at a Buddhist temple, the devout also light incense.*

with a churning sound: and when they lifted up the spear again, the brine dripping down from the tip of the spear piled up and became an island. Descending from the heavens, Izanagi and Izanami married on this island and erected a heavenly pillar and a spacious palace.

Discovering that their bodies were differently formed, Izanagi asked his spouse Izanami if she was agreeable to giving birth to the land. When she agreed, he suggested, 'Then let us, you and me, walk in a circle around this heavenly pillar and meet and join'. After several failures, they started to bear children, which are the islands of Japan.

There have been various interpretations of this ritual of circling around the heavenly pillar. Scholars of the late Edo period (from the 18th century to the early 19th century) regarded the pillar simply as the symbol of the phallus. It clearly has links with the European maypole, which is believed to capture the vital powers latent in a tree, and also with the ancient Japanese belief that processions round tall trees are needed to summon down the deities who live in the heavens or on high mountains.

Until the scholar Motoori Norinaga discovered the importance of the *Kojiki* in the 18th century, it was regarded as far inferior to its contemporary, the *Nihon-shoki*, a history book completed in 720AD, eight years after the presentation of the *Kojiki*. The *Nihon-shoki* is in many ways more accessible than the *Kojiki* as it presents its material in a more detached way. The *Kojiki*, on the other hand, invites the readers to have strong

BELOW *Noh drama began in the Heian period (8th–12th centuries), was highly developed by the 14th century, and is still very popular today.*

sympathy with the myths, and does not seem to care much about the coherence and logic of the stories it includes. Norinaga, however, thought that the very simplicity and incoherence of the *Kojiki* is what its compilers intended, aiming to recreate the religious sense of ancient Japanese through a careful organization of prose and poetry. It is important to read the myths with imagination and faith, rather than looking for rational explanations to the stories.

When the *Kojiki* was written, the influence of China was starting to be apparent everywhere. The legal system, the arts and literature were strongly affected. As the influence of Buddhism spread from China and Asia in the 6th century and became the dominant belief among the aristocracy, the *Kojiki* was important in recording Japanese life before foreign influences took too great a hold. The

book portrayed an image of life filled with a strong sense of the unity of Man with nature and god, and the unity between people through simple rituals. It also aimed to bring about clear self-consciousness through having a lucid image of the past to overcome the crisis of national identity, in some ways a crisis similar to the one Japan is facing now.

In the book, purity (or growth power) is exemplified by the story of Yamato-takeru. The opposite concept of *kaegare* (or pollution) is illustrated by the story of Izanami's death:

THE HEARTH OF YOMI

After giving birth to numerous islands and other features of nature

BELOW Yakushi-nyorai (Lord of the Eastern Paradise) shown here flanked by two attendants in the Yakushiji temple in Nara. The gilt statues were blackened in a fire in 1528.

– waterfalls, mountains, trees, herbs and the wind – Izanami died of a terrible fever. Izanagi followed her to Yomi, the land of the dead but was too late: she had already eaten at the hearth of Yomi. She asked Izanagi to wait for her patiently as she discussed with the gods whether she could return, but he could not. He threw down the comb he was wearing and set light to it, and then he entered the hall. What he saw was dreadful:

'Maggots were squirming and roaring in Izanami's corpse. In her head was Great-Thunder; in her breast was Fire-Thunder; in her belly was Black-Thunder; in her genitals was Crack-Thunder; in her right hand was Earth-Thunder; in her left foot was Sounding–Thunder; in her right foot was Reclining-Thunder. Altogether there were eight thunder deities.'

As can be seen from the above description of the land of the dead, ancient Japanese ideas about death and the afterlife contained no thought of a final judgement. The land of the dead, Yomi, is the land of filth and uncleanliness rather than that of horror or punishment. By eating from the hearth of Yomi, Izanami can no longer return to the land of the living. Norinaga considered that this was because food cooked with the fire of Yomi became impure. A simpler interpretation is that Izanami, having eaten the food of Yomi, had become a person of Yomi. The idea that one cannot return home after having eaten the food of the afterlife – or even of a foreign land – is a common one throughout the world. In the final passage of the relationship between Izanami and Izanagi, the concept of mortality for mankind is introduced. The use of peaches as a weapon is a sign of Chinese influence on the *Kojiki*. In China, peaches and peach trees have from antiquity been used to dispel demons and evil spirits. The peach is also often used as a symbol of longevity (see page 45).

DEATH COMES TO THE WORLD

Izanagi was frightened by the sight of Izanami, and he turned and fled. Shamed by his actions, Izanami sends the hags of Yomi to pursue him, but he evades them using magic tricks. When Izanagi arrived at the border between the land of the living and Yomi, he attacked his pursuers with three peaches he had found nearby. They all turned and fled. Then Izanagi said to the peaches: 'Just as you have

saved me, when any of the race of mortal men fall into painful straits and suffer in anguish, then do you save them also.'

Finally, Izanami herself came in pursuit of Izanagi. He pulled a huge boulder across the pass from Yomi to the land of the living, and Izanagi and Izanami stood facing each other on either side of the boulder. Izanami then said: 'O my beloved husband, if you do thus, I will each day strangle to death 1,000 of the populace of your country.' To this Izanagi replied: 'O my beloved spouse, if you do this, I will each day build 1,500 parturition huts' meaning that this number of people would be born.

Thus the marriage of Izanami and Izanagi brings the natural world into existence, and their separation, or 'divorce', is the beginning of mortality.

On his return to the land of the living, Izanagi rids himself of the sullying effects of his descent into the underworld by undergoing purification.

'He arrived at the plain by the river-mouth, where he took off his clothes and the articles worn on his body. As each item was flung on to the ground, a deity came into existence. And as Izanagi entered the water to wash himself, yet more gods were created.'

Izanagi's act of cleansing (*misogi*) shows how vital force can be recovered by purification. In the same way that rice growing follows a cycle in which both the land the the people become exhausted, and are then revitalized by water or a period of rest, so Izanagi regains his strength and vitality by taking off his heavy garments and immersing himself in the waters. Water is a potent symbol in many scenes of everyday life in Japan today. For example, as soon as you take a seat in a *sushi* restaurant in Tokyo, the table will be wiped with a white cloth soaked in water. This has little to do with hygiene, rather it is an act of purification before rice is eaten.

LEFT *Large hanging scroll painting of a waterfall by Maruyama Okyo (1733–1795), said to have been commissioned by an abbott who felt bereft without an actual waterfall to contemplate.*

LEFT *In order to make a wish come true the Japanese buy good luck Daruma dolls and paint in one of the eyes. If their wish is granted, they paint in the other as a sign of gratitude.*

RIGHT *To the untutored eye, it is very difficult to differentiate between Japanese and Chinese painting: these are in fact three of a set of eight album leaves attributed to the Chinese artist Gong Xian (fl. 1656–82), ink and slight colour on paper. Compare this to the Japanese paintings on pages 100 and 107. The long and complex relationship between the two countries has been both tragic and fruitful.*

Nothing evokes the feeling of clarity more for Japanese than seeing a fall of water against a mountain setting, preferably with a small shrine at the base of the waterfall.

Finally, when Izanagi washes his eyes, he brings into being three of the most important gods in the Japanese pantheon – the sun goddess, the moon god and Susano, the storm god. The brother/sister pair of Amaterasu, the sun goddess, and Tukiyomi, the moon god, are respectively responsible for day and night. Of the many stories recounted of Amaterasu, the tale of her withdrawal of labour, is very well known. Amaterasu and Susano had fallen out after Susano played a trick on the sun goddess which resulted in the destruction of her rice fields. Amaterasu retaliated by withdrawing into a cave, thus casting the world into darkness. There she stayed until a goddess, egged on by other deities, performed a riotous dance outside the cave. Unable to contain her curiosity, Amaterasu emerged and caught sight of her reflection in a mirror that the gods had suspended from a tree. Since then the world has experienced the normal cycle of day and night.

Amaterasu is supposed to be the direct ancestor of the Japanese imperial family; a mirror forms part of

BELOW *Shigisan scroll from the Kamakura period (12th–13th centuries) depicting scenes from the lives of ordinary people; agriculture, represented by the bullock, is never far away.*

the imperial regalia. The obedience that was owed to the emperor finds an echo in the veneration of the sun goddess. Amaterasu occupies a key position among the huge number of Shinto gods (by some counts, more than eight million) of which the mythological creatures known as *tengu* are amongst the most ancient.

PART HUMAN, PART BIRD

*T*engu are believed to inhabit trees in mountainous areas, particularly pines and cryptomerias. Part human and part bird, they are sometimes shown wearing cloaks of feathers or leaves, and often sport a small, black hat. *Tengu* love to play tricks, although this stems more from a sense of mischief than evil. Often, however, they fail to appreciate it when the joke is on them! A boy taunted a *tengu* by claiming he was able to see into heaven by using a hollow piece of bamboo as a telescope. The *tengu*, overcome with curiosity, agreed to swap his cloak of invisibility for the stick of bamboo. When he found he had been deceived, the *tengu* took his revenge by causing the boy to fall into an icy river.

Oni are supposed to have come to Japan from China along with the Buddhist faith. They are horned devils, often of giant size, with three fingers and toes. Sometimes they also have three eyes. Whereas tengu are playful, *oni* are usually cruel, generally not very bright and often lecherous, as the following stories show:

ONI AND KAPPAS

*M*omotaro, revered for his nobility of spirit and accomplishments in battle, was born into a peach. A

childless couple found the peach floating in a mountain stream, and on cutting it open, revealed a tiny baby boy. They named him Momotaro, which means 'peach child' and brought him up as their own son. When he was 15, Momotaro decided to repay his adopted parents and their neighbours for their generosity. A number of *oni* inhabited an island nearby and were making raids on the mainland to steal treasure and terrorize the population. Taking three rice cakes from his mother, Momotaro set off on his mission. On his way he met a dog, a

ABOVE Dotaku, *a mysterious bronze object, probably though not certainly a bell, now held by the Kobe City Museum. Its ritual significance or purpose can only be guessed at.*

111

pheasant and a monkey who each agreed to accompany him in return for a rice cake. The band of four took a boat to the island of the *oni*, where they found a number of girls being held captive after being kidnapped and raped. With the help of his companions, Momotaro launched an attack on the *oni* stronghold, and killed all the supernatural beings. The boat was then piled high with the stolen treasure and the prisoners released. Momotaro returned home in triumph, and was able to ensure that his parents lived out their lives in comfort.

Another diminutive hero is Issun Boshi, whose name means 'Little One Inch':

After many years of marriage, Issun Boshi's parents had not managed to conceive, so they prayed to the gods for a child, even one just as long as the end of a finger. The gods took them at their word, and Issun Boshi was born. At the age of 15 (a significant birthday for tiny heroes, it seems) Issun Boshi set off on a trip to Kyoto, the capital. He took with him his parents' gifts of a rice bowl, a pair of chopsticks and a needle stuck in a sheath of bamboo. He travelled by river, using the bowl as a boat and a chopstick as a punt. On arriving in the city, Issun Boshi found himself employment in the service of a noble family. He worked hard for a number of years and entered the affections of his employers. One day Issun Boshi accompanied the daughter of the house to the temple. On their way two giant oni leapt out in ambush. Issun Boshi tried to draw attention to himself, thus enabling the girl to escape. When one of the oni swallowed him, Issun Boshi drew his needle from its scabbard and began to stab the oni's stomach. He then clambered his way up the giant's gullet, stabbing with his weapon all the time. When he reached the mouth, the oni spat him out as fast as he could. The other oni lunged for Issun Boshi, but he jumped into its eye were he continued to wield his miniature sword.

As the hapless devils retreated, one of them dropped a mallet. Recognizing this as a lucky instrument, Issun Boshi and the girl struck it on the ground and made a wish. Immediately, Issun Boshi grew to normal size and was clothed in the armour of a samurai, whose attributes he had already shown himself to possess. On the couple's return, the father happily gave his permission for them to wed. Issun Boshi proved himself to be a devoted husband and brought his aged parents to Kyoto to share in his good fortune.

According to some, the *kappa* is a creature descended from the monkey messenger of the river god. Resembling a monkey, but with fish scales or a tortoise shell instead of fur, the child-

BELOW *Heian shrine in Kyoto; the pagoda structure is an adaptation of Chinese architecture.*

ABOVE *Picture of a* kappa *emerging from a pool; from the scroll painting* Bakemonojin, The Compendium of Ghosts *(1788).*

sized *kappa* is yellow or green in colour. They inhabit rivers, ponds and lakes and have a hollow in the top of the head in which water is carried. If this water is spilled, the *kappa* is then deprived of his magical powers. Like vampires, *kappa* feed on human blood, although they are also known to consume the blood of horses and cattle. As well as blood, *kappa* have a taste for cucumbers, and can be persuaded not to harm humans if a cucumber inscribed with the names and ages of the members of the family is thrown into the water in which they live. The ability to keep a promise is a distinguishing and appealing feature of *kappas*, as is their politeness. This is often their downfall, as when they bow down, the water spills from the indentation in the head causing their strength to disappear.

A *kappa* who resembled a small child would ask passers-by to play pull-

BELOW *Play performed at Sansen-in temple at Ohara, a mountainous area dotted with quiet villages, depicting the ancient gods and heroes.*

finger, and then drag its victims down into the pond in which it lived. A horseback rider agreed to play the game, but when their hands were locked, urged his horse into a gallop. As the water spilled from the *kappa*'s head, it begged for mercy. In return for its freedom, the *kappa* promised to teach the rider how to mend broken bones. On being released, the kappa kept its word and taught the rider all it knew. The knowledge handed over by the *kappa* was passed down through generations of the rider's family.

BUDDHIST INFLUENCE

Buddhism was introduced to Japan from Korea in the middle of the 6th century. The first, and one of the most profound texts on Buddhism, *Giso,* appeared as early as the 7th century and was written by Shotoku Taishi, a member of the imperial family who gave much support to the new religion. As is clear from the stories of the *Kojiki,* Shinto is a cult in which the spirit of every thing is worshipped, without a systematic structure or doctrine. Life after death is accepted, but early Shinto contained no moral teaching, or concept of reward or punishment after death. The term Shinto, which means 'Way of the Gods', only came into use after the introduction of Buddhism when it became necessary to differentiate between the two systems of belief.

Although there was opposition to the spread of Buddhism, by the middle of the 8th century the two religions were closely intertwined. Kobo Taishi (774–834) introduced the doctrine of Ryobu, or 'Shinto with two faces', which permitted a compromise to be reached. For the next 1,000 years, Buddhist temples would contain Shinto shrines and Shinto deities would be regarded as Buddhist guardians. Buddhist monks conducted the services at Shinto shrines (except at Izumo and Ise, where Amaterasu's shrine still exists). This happy coexistence came to an end with the beginning of the Meiji Restoration in 1868.

SOUL OF THE BUTTERFLY

This charming tale combines the Buddhist virtue of filial piety with the Shinto belief that all things, inanimate and animate, have a spirit.

A young man and woman who shared a great passion for gardening were married. They lived together in great happiness, their love for their plants only surpassed by the pleasure they took in one another's company. Late in life they had a son, who fortunately inherited his parents' interest in plants. The couple died from old age a few days apart, while their son was still a youth. The boy took over the responsibility for the garden,

ABOVE *In front of the main building, marking off the area of the gods, hangs the shrine* nawa, *which is made from rope that has been ritually purified.*

BELOW *A Netsuke rat, one of the 12 animals of the zodiac, another of the many examples of Japanese borrowings from China. Netsuke are exquisitely carved ornaments originally used as fasteners or brooches.*

tending it with the care and devotion that he had learned from his parents. In the spring that followed their death, he observed each day two butterflies in the garden. One night he dreamed that his mother and father were wandering round their beloved garden, inspecting the plants they knew so well to see how they were faring in the boy's care. Suddenly, the old couple turned into a pair of butterflies, but continued their round of the garden, alighting on each flower in turn. The next day the pair of butterflies were still in the garden, and the boy knew that they contained the souls of his parents who were continuing to derive pleasure from their life's work.

It was during the Kamakura period (12th and 13th centuries) that a truly Japanese Buddhism emerged. Honen and his disciple Shinran were responsible for the spreading of the Jodo school among ordinary people, and can thus take credit for its immense popularity ever since. Jodo made Buddhism accessible by arguing that one could achieve enlightenment by abandoning oneself to Amida Buddha, and popular Buddhism embraced many gods, including the seven gods of fortune:

THE SEVEN GODS

*H*otei can be distinguished by his enormous pot belly, which overhangs his lower garments, but western assumptions of greed would be quite wrong, however. For Hotei's protruding stomach is a symbol of a soul that has achieved serenity through Buddhism, and an indication of its owner's contentment and good nature.

The god of longevity, *Jurojin*, is always depicted with a white beard and shown in the company of a crane, tortoise or deer – which are themselves symbols of long life. He carries a staff from which hangs a scroll that contains the wisdom of the world.

Fukurokuju is easily identified by his odd appearance. He has a very long and narrow head, which is combined with a short and squat body and legs. He, also, is associated with the desirable attributes of long life and wisdom.

Daikoku is regarded as the patron of farmers. He is often shown seated on rice bales, which are sometimes being eaten away beneath him by rats. To this, Daikoku responds with his customary good humour as he is so wealthy that he can afford not to be perturbed! He carries a mallet with which he is able to grant wishes.

Another Buddhist god, who is sometimes seen as a god of wealth also, is *Bishamon*. He is always portrayed in full armour, carrying a spear in one hand and a miniature pagoda in the other – thus showing that he combines the virtues of a warrior and a missionary.

The qualities exemplified by the god *Ebisu* are those of honest toil. The patron of traders and fishermen,

only the latter activity identifies him – he is usually shown holding a fishing rod and his catch, a sea bream.

The last of the seven is the goddess *Benten*. She occupies an important position among the group for she is associated with the sea. Many shrines to Benten are by the sea or on islands, and she is often portrayed riding a dragon or sea serpent. Benten is an example of the ideals of feminine deportment and accomplishment in the arts, and is often pictured playing a *biwa*, a mandolin-like instrument of which she is fond.

The Kamakura period was the heyday of Japanese chivalry, when the shoguns employed the samurai as their bodyguards. The samurai, who were not aristocrats but mostly came from farming backgrounds, were well acquainted with the harsh realities of life. They found in Zen Buddhism – which was introduced to Japan at the same time as Jodo – another route to the heart of Buddhism. The directness of Zen, 'the spiritual cult of steel', held great appeal for the samurai warriors, who had neither the time nor the inclination to undertake long study or indulge in abstract argument in order to achieve enlightenment. The

ABOVE *Netsuke showing the seven gods of fortune in their ship.*

RIGHT *Ink on paper painting by the monk Hakuin (1685–1768) of Bodhidharma, founder of the Zen sect.*

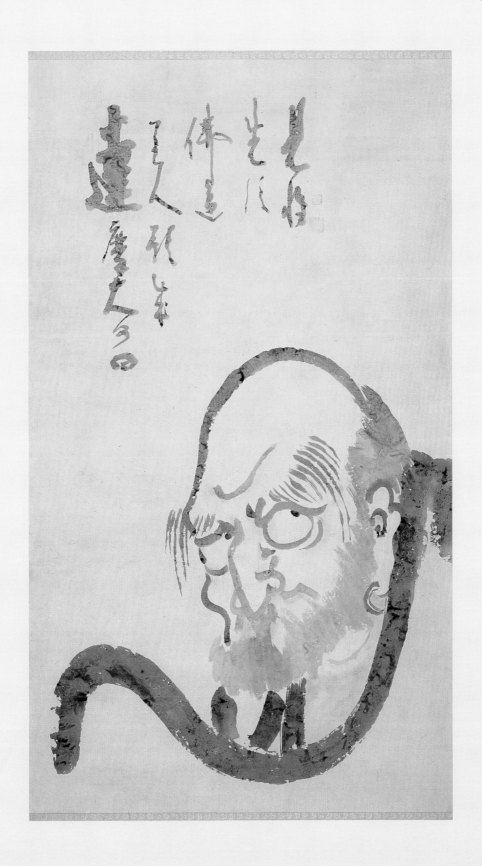

RIGHT *Pine trees, of
which there are many
varieties, have a
particular significance
in Japanese painting.
Because the leaves do
not fall or change
colour, they have come
to symbolize longevity;
(ink on paper by
Tohaku Hasegawa,
1539–1616).*

purpose of Zen is to move beyond the realm of the intellect. Zen rejects the use of words to explain experience as mere substitute for reality. Zen is taught through a series of short, elliptical dialogues (*mondo*) which have been described as a duel between master and pupil, another reason perhaps for their appeal to the warriors. When Joshu was asked about the fundamental principle of Buddhism, he replied, 'The cypress-tree in the courtyard in front of you'. 'You are talking of an objective symbol,' said the pupil. 'No, I am not talking of an objective symbol.' 'Then,' asked the monk again, 'What is the ultimate principle of Buddhism?' 'The cypress-tree in the courtyard in front of you,' again replied Joshu.

Zen stresses the one-ness of man and nature and herein lies the reason why it has become the dominant school of Buddhism in Japan. The myths of the *Kojiki* demonstrate that familiarity with and reverence towards the natural world that are so strong in the Japanese tradition. Not only is there no antagonism between Zen and the native Shinto sensibilities, but the different beliefs actually enhance one another. After being accepted by the samurai class, Zen started to permeate every single aspect

BELOW View of the extensive gardens of Tofukugi temple, Kyoto.

of Japanese life. It is impossible to talk about Japanese culture without mentioning Zen. Architecture (tea-houses), poetry (*haiku*), sports (archery and swordmanship), painting (brush painting), gardening (stone gardens), theatre (*Noh*), ceramics and food – all these areas of creative activity are heavily influenced by Zen.

Shinto architecture gave concrete form to the concept of purity, as exemplified in the stories of the *Kojiki* and its simplicity and lack of abstraction also follow the precepts of Zen. Ise Shrine, the central shrine of Shintoism, is situated in the deep forest beside a river whose water is crystal clear. The shrine occupies a vast area. The buildings are in the shape of a rice-storage house, and all are made of bare wood, without paint or ornament, built on white pebble stones. Clear, straight lines dominate, with a few curves on the rooves. All the buildings, together with their various contents, are rebuilt every 20 years, thus ensuring that the necessary skills to make them are transferred from generation to generation. This tradition goes back to ancient times. When they are newly built, the bare wood

ABOVE *White sand and rocks laid out in the garden of the 15th-century Ryonji temple; Zen purity.*

RIGHT *Miyajima (shrine island) near Hiroshima; since time immemorial, neither births nor burials nor dogs are permitted on the island.*

BELOW *Calligraphic poem from the late Heian period; the flourishing of calligraphy in Japan is also influenced by Zen Buddhism.*

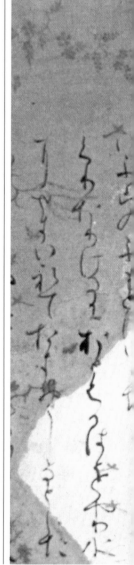

RIGHT *Young girl
assistants, known as*
Miko, *participating in
Shinto ritual at Ise
Grand Shrine.*

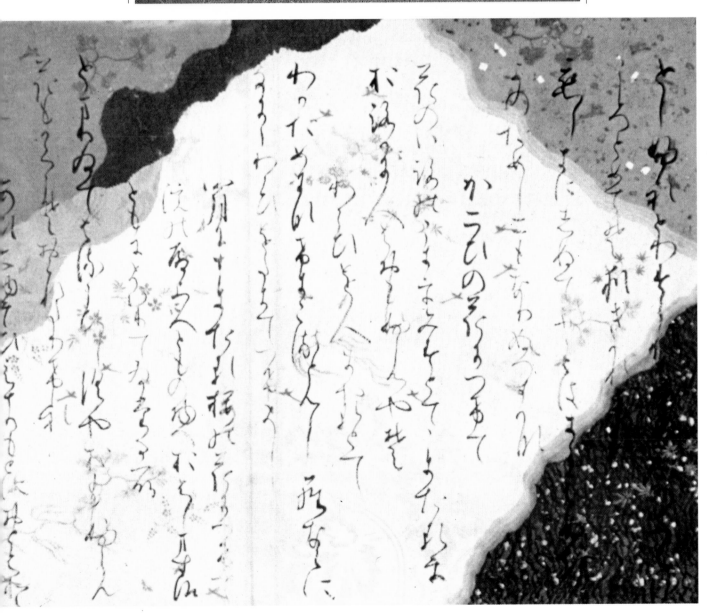

RIGHT *The Golden pavilion of Kinkakuji temple, completed in 1955, an exact replica of a 14th-century villa that was destroyed by fire.*

RIGHT *Jacket from a Noh costume woven in a style that imitates a Chinese technique.*

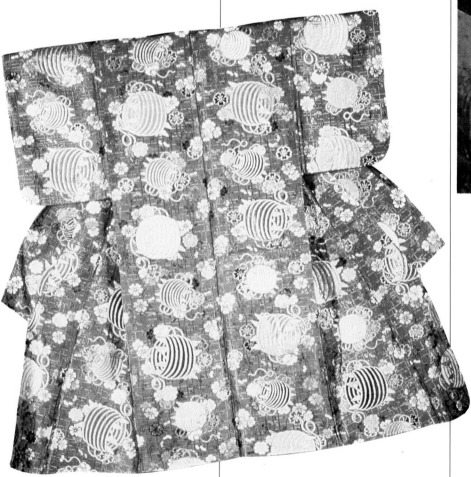

shines gold in the quiet, dark forest. The shrine shows us what an architect can express employing only purely functional lines. Ise shrine is the prototype of later Japanese architecture: Katsura imperial villa, which was made in the 17th century, has much in common with Ise shrine. This building, which was designed by Kobori Enshu, exemplifies the Japanese style of simplicity and functionality, and an intense affinity with natural form and material.

The high points for artistic activity in Japanese history – the Kamakura and Muromachi periods – gave full expression to the spirit of Zen. But the manner and form that it took harked back to ancient times, the times so lovingly recorded in the *Kojiki*: sculptures of angry Buddhist gods remind us of Yamato-takeru, and the costumes of Noh plays display elegant designs that represent the plants that grow on the mountains and blossom in the fields where deities of the *Kojiki* once lived.

ABOVE *Sliding door painting from Chisyaku-in temple, Kyoto; the contemplation of, and respect for, the natural world is central both to Shintoism and Buddhism. Shintoism, with its acceptance that every natural thing, be it a man or a plum tree, has a kami or spirit, encouraged the proliferation of mythical stories, and its complex relationship with Buddhism further enriched and invigorated Japanese mythology.*

123

Bibliography

CHINESE MYTHOLOGY

Chinese Mythology (Library of the World's Myths and Legends) by Anthony Christie. Newns Books, London, 1968
Dragons, Gods and Spirits from Chinese Mythology by Tao Tao Liu Saunders; illustrations by Johnny Pau. Peter Lowe: Eurobook Ltd, 1980
Classical Chinese Myths, edited and translated by Jan and Yvonne Walls; illustrations by Guo Huai-ren. Joint Publishing Co., Hong Kong, 1984
Monkey by Wu Cheng'en; translated by Arthur Waley. Unwin Paperbacks, London, 1984
Myths and Legends of China by E.T.C. Werner, London, 1922
A Dictionary of Chinese Symbols: Hidden Symbols in Chinese Life and Thought by Wolfram Eberhard. Routledge, London, 1988

INDIAN MYTHOLOGY

Seasons of Splendour – Tales, Myths and Legends of India by Madhur Jaffrey; illustrations by Michael Foreman. Pavilion Books, London, 1985
Indian Myth and Legend by Donald A. Mackenzie. The Gresham Publishing Company
Demons, Gods and Holy Men from Indian Myths and Legends by Shahrukh Husain; illustrations by Durga Prasad Das. Eurobook, 1987

The Dance of Shiva and Other Tales from India by Oroon Ghosh. Signet Classics, New York, 1965
Hindu Myths, translation and introduction by Wendy Doniger O'Flaherty. Penguin Books, New York, 1975
The Sword and the Flute by David R. Kinsley. University of California Press, Berkeley, 1977
Myths and Symbols in Indian Art and Civilization by Heinrich Zimmer. Harper Torchbooks, New York, 1962
The Indian Way by John M Koller. Macmillan Publishing Co. Inc., New York, 1982

JAPANESE MYTHOLOGY

Continuity and Change by Ichiro Hori. University of Chicago Press, 1968
At the Fountain-head of Japan by Jean Herbert. George Allen & Unwin, London, 1967
The Kami Way by Sokyo Ono. Bridgeway Press, 1962
Japanese Religion: Unity and Diversity (The Religious Life of Man Series) by Byron Earhart. Wadsworth Publishing Company, California, 1982
On Understanding Japanese Religion by Joseph M. Kitagawa. Princeton University Press, Princeton, 1987
Living by Zen by Daisetz Suzuki. Rider & Company, London, 1969
What is Zen? by D. Suzuki. The Buddhist Society, London, 1971
Zen Culture by Thomas Hoover. Routledge, London, 1977
The Kojiki, translated with an Introduction and Notes by Donald L. Philippi. University of Tokyo Press, 1968

Index

Page references in *italic* refer to captions.

A

Adi Granth, 53
Agni, 56, *56*, 76, 78
Ajanta, India, *8*
Emperor Akihito, 91, 98
Altair, 31
Amaterasu, *106*, 110–11, 114
Amida Buddha, 116
ancestor worship, 16
Aolai Mountain, 43–4
apsaras, *13*
architecture, 120, 123
artistic influences, 11, 17
Asi-gara, 102
Asuka period, 96
asura, 80–1
Avalokitsvara, 42

B

Princess Badr i Munir, 84, 86–7
Bakemonojin, The Compendium of Ghosts, 112
Balaram, 74–6
de Bary, T: *Sources of Indian Tradition*, 60
Benazir, 84, 86–7
Bengal, 60
Benten, 116
Bhaghavad Gita, 54, 76
Bhumi, *71*
Bishamon, 116
Black-Thunder, 106
Blue-Throat *see* Shiva

Boddhisattva, 42, *42*, 59, 80, *80*, 81
Bodhidharma (Hakuin), *116*
Book of Changes *see I Ching*
Brahma, 53–4, *54*, 58, 60, *81*
Brahmani bull, 56
the Buddha, *8*, 9, 18, 46–7, *46*, 52, 71, 78, 79, *79*, 81, 84, 88
Buddhism, 10–11, *10*, *13*, 15, 17–18, 39, 52–3, 59, 79, 84, 105, 114–16, 119–20
Buddhist cave temples, *13*
Bundako theatre, *102*
Bundi, *51*
burial rituals, 52, 91
Burmese art, *59*

C

the calendar, 38, *38*
calligraphy, *120*
caste system, 10
ceramics, *21*, *24*, 36, 44
ceremonial pieces, *14*
chaityas, *8*
Chang, E, 28–31, *30*, *39*
Chang Kuo Lao, *34*
Chinese art, *17*, *23*, *24*, 28, *32*, *34*, *47*
Chinese mythology, 13–47, 54

Chisyaku-in temple, *123*
Chola sculpture, *54*, 64
Confucius, 15–16
Confucianism, 15–16
Cosmic Egg, *54*
Cowell, E B *ed*: Jataka: *Stories of Buddha's Former Births*, 84
Crack-Thunder, 106
the creation, *54*, 56, 58, 60, 103

D

Daikoku, 116
Daksha, 65–7
Daruma dolls, *108*
Dazu, China, *9*
death, *15*, 17–18, 39, 52, 91
Devaki, 72
Diamond Sutra scroll, *46*
Dijun, 27–8
Divine Couple, 63
Diwali festival, *51*, 71, 89
Diya, 24
Dotaku, *111*
dragon dances, 38, *38*
Dragon King of the Eastern Sea, 44–5
dragon-boats, 38
dragons, 36–8, *38*
drama, 48–9, 98, *102*, *104*, *113*, 120, 123
Dravidian tribe, 52

Dunhuang, China, *6*, 46
Dunhuang cave paintings, *10*, *11*
Durga, 68, 69
Dussehra, 88
Dwapara Yuga, 58

E

Earth-Thunder, 106
Ebisu, 116
Edo period, 99, 103
embroidery, *26*, 30, *31*, 36
Enshu, Kobori *123*

F

family unity, 15–16, 38
fengshui, 17
fertility symbols, 8–9
festivals, *10*, 38, *38*, 88, 89, *89*, 92, 100
Fire-Thunder, 106
Firoz Shah, 87
flooding, 35–6, 38–40, 42
Forbidden City, Peking, *23*
foreign influences, 14–15
Forster, E M: *A Passage to India*, 65
four Ages of Man, 58
Fukei (Tokuwaka), *102*
Fukurokuju, 116
funerals *see* burial rituals

Fusang, 27
Fuxi, *21*, 23–24
Fuxi dynasty, 9, 14

G

Ganesh, 63, 67, *67*, 69
Ganges, 60
Garden of Immortal Peaches, 45
Garuda, *51*
Gautama Buddha, 79, 79
geomancers, 38, *39*
Gion festival, *10*, *92*, 100
Giso, 114
God of the East *see* Dijun
god of fire *see* Agni
God of Literature *see* Wenchang
god of longevity *see* Jurogin
God of War *see* Guandi
goddess of mercy *see* Guan Yin
Goddess of the Sun *see* Xihe
goddess of weaving, 32
Gokul, 72–3
Golden Guardians, 47
Gong Xian, *17*, *109*
Gonggong, 24–6
Gopis, 75
granddaughter of heaven, 32
graves *see* tombs

Great Sage, equal of Heaven, 45
Great Wall of China, 28
Great Yu, 36, 42, 44
Great-Thunder, 106
Guan Yin, 42, 47
see also Avalokitsvara
Guan Zhong, 40, 42
Guandi, 40, *40*, 42
Guanyin, 94
Gujarat, India, *57*
Gun, 35, 36, 42
Guru Nanak, 52

H

haiku poetry, 102, 120
Hakuin: *Bodhidharma*, *116*
Hall of Prayer, Temple of Heaven, *22*
Han dynasty, 15, 36, 40
Haniwa, *92*, *100*
Hanuman, 76, *77*, *77*, 78
Harihari, *61*
Hasegawa, *118*
Heavenly Maidens, 32
Heian period, 104, *120*
Heian shrine, *112*
hell *see* the underworld
Hinayana Buddhism *see* Theravada Buddhism
Hindu religion, *9*, 52–4, 60, 71, 76, 84
Hinoshina shrine, *95*

Hirohito, Emperor, 91, 98
Hokusai of Tago-ono-ura, 99
Honen, 115
Horyuji temple, 96
Hotei, 116
house gods, 39, 40, 40
Hymn to the Cosmic Person, 56

I

I Ching, 20
Indian art, 8, 52–4, 56–7, 66–8, 70–2, 74–6, 79, 81, 86
Indian mythology, 51–89
The Indian Way, 58
Indra, 56, 81
Indrajit, 78
Ise shrine, 120, 121, 123
Islam see Muslim religion
Issun Boshi, 112
ivories, 34
Izanagi, 9, 103–4, 106–7, 110
Izanami, 9, 103–7
Izumo shrine, 93

J

Jade Emperor, 39, 45, 46
Jain religion, 7, 52, 52, 53, 57, 58, 60
Japanese art, 91, 92, 97, 107, 112, 116, 118, 123
Japanese mythology, 91–123
Jataka tales, 53, 80, 84
Jidai festival, 103
Jodo, 115–16
Joshu, 119
Journey to the West see Xi you ji
Jurojin, 116
justice, 40

K

Kabuku dance theatre, 98
kaegare, 105
Kagura dances, 106
Kali, 69, 69, 70
Kali Yuga, 58
Kaliya, 74
Kalkin, 70, 71
kalpas, 58
Kamaskura period, 110, 115–6, 123
kamis, 123
Kangra, India, 72
Kangxi, 21
Kans of Mathura, 72–6
kappas, 112, 112, 113, 114
Karttikeya, 63
Kasuge shrine, 106

Katsura imperial villa, 123
Keeper of the Heavenly Horses, 45
Emperor Keiko, 95
Kinkakuji temple, 122
Kinsley, D R:
The Sword and the Flute, 74
Kitchen God, 40
Kobori Enshu, 123
the Kojiki, 91, 93, 94, 95, 96, 102–6, 114, 119–20
Koller, John M:
The Indian Way, 58
Konarak, India, 9
Kongfuzi see Confucius
Korin, Ogata, 91
Krishna, 54, 71–2, 72, 73–4, 74, 75–6, 75
Krita Yuga, 58
Kumbh-Mela, 88
Kwannon, 94
Kyoto, Japan, 7, 92, 103

L

Lakshmi, 51, 51, 64, 71
Lamaistic Buddhism, 59
Landscape for Four Seasons (sesshu), 92
Lanka, Kingdom of, 77–8, 89
Lau Tzu, 16
Laozi, 16, 45
Leshan Buddha, China 18
Lhasa, Tibet, 8
Liao dynasty, 42
lingam, 64, 64
Little One Inch see Issun Boshi
lohans, 43
Longmen, China, 13
Longmen cave temples, 13
Lord of the Dance see Shiva
Shiva Nataraja
Lord of the Eastern Paradise, 105
Lord of the Underworld see Yama

M

Mahabalipuram, India, 6
the Mahabharata, 9, 52, 54, 76
Maharashtra, 89
Mahavira, 52
Mahayana Buddhism, 59
Mahisha, 68
Manchu tribes, 14
Mandara, 64
Manu, 71–2
Mao Tse Tung, 13

Mardana, 52
Marhukh, 84, 87
marriage, 86
Master Kong see Confucius
Matale, Sri Lanka, 9
Mathura, India, 7
Matsya, 71–2, 72
Queen Maya, 78, 79, 81
Mazu, 42
Meng Qiang nu, 28
Milky Way, 31
Ming dynasty, 16, 34, 42, 45
Mir Hasan, 84
misogi, 107
Miyajima, 120
modern life, 94, 95
Momotaro, 111, 112
mondos, 119
Monkey, 43–7, 43, 47
monkey god see Hanuman
moon god see Tukiyomi
Motoori Norinaga, 104–6
Mount Buzhon, 25
Mount Hemavat, 72
Mount Ibuki, 102
Mount Kunlun, 18, 24, 29
Mountain of the Soul, 47
Mughal art, 84, 86, 89
Mughal empire, 84
Muromachi period, 123
Muslim religion, 52, 53, 84

N

Najm un Nisa, 86–7
Nanda, 72–4
Nandi, 63, 64, 66
Narayana see Brahma
nawas, 115
Netsuke, 115, 116
Nihal Chand:
Radha, 75
Nihon-shoki, 104
Nilakantha see Shiva
Nobo, 102
Noh plays 102, 104, 120, 122, 123
Nugua, 21, 22–4, 25–6
Nugua dynasty, 9, 14

O

O'Flaherty, Wendy:
The Origins of Evil in Indian Mythology, 54
Okyo, Manuyama, 107
oni, 111–12
Opo-usu, 95
oral traditions, 51
Oto-tatiban-pime, 99
Ox Star, 32

P

Pagoda of the Six

Harmonies, China, 33
Pangu, 20–1, 43
Parashurama, 71
Parsvanartha, 52
Parvati, 63, 66, 67, 69
A Passage to India (Forster), 65
Patoona, 73
Peking, China, 16, 22, 23
Peng Meng, 31
phoenix, 36–7, 36
Pigsy, 43, 43, 47
poetry, 102, 120, 120
Prajapati, 54
Purusha, 56, 56

Q

Queen Mother of the West see Xiwangmu
Qing dynasty, 14, 18, 21, 26, 28, 40, 44

R

Radha, 72, 74, 75
Rahu, 9
Rahula, 79
Raja Savant Singh, 75
Rajasthan, India, 54
Rama, 71, 76, 76, 77–8, 88, 89
Rama-lila, 89
the Ramayana, 9, 52, 54, 60, 76
Ravana, 76–8, 88, 89
Reclining-Thunder, 106
Record of Ancient Things see the Kojiki
Register of the Dead, 45
reincarnation, 10–11, 17–18
The Remover of Obstacles see Ganesh
Rengyoin temple, 94
Rig Veda, 54, 56
Romance of the Three Kingdoms, 42
Ryobu, 114
Ryonji temple, 120

S

Sagamu, 98–9
Sampati, 77
Samsara, 64
samurai, 116
Sanci torso, 80
Sansen-in temple, 113
Sarasvati, 60, 60
Sati, 65–6, 69
the seasons, 9–10, 17, 29, 54
Sesshu, 92, 97
Shang dynasty, 14, 14
Shangdi, 39
Shigisan art, 110
Shinran, 115
Shintoism, 10, 91, 93, 96, 98, 111, 114, 119, 120, 121, 123
Shiva, 53, 60, 61–6,

62–7, 69, 70
Shiva Nataraja, 64
shoguns, 116
Shou, 18
Shoulao, 32
Prince Siddhartha, 79
Sikh religion, 52
Sinhika, 77
Sita, 76–8, 89
social structure, 8, 10
Son of Heaven, 36
Sotatsu, Tawaraya:
Waves at Matsushima, 99
Sounding-Thunder, 106
Sources of Indian Tradition (de Bary), 60
Sri Lanka, 59
Steatite seal, 56
storm god see Susano
stupas, 6, 81
suan ye school, 24
King Suddhodana, 79
Summer (Gong Xian), 17
Sumo wrestling, 96, 97
Sun see Monkey
sun goddess see Amaterasu
Surabhi, 64
Surasa, 77
Susano, 110
sushi, 107, 110
Sword and the Flute (Kinsley), 74
symbolism, 8–9

T

Tagi, 102
Tang dynasty, 23, 28, 34, 35, 39
Tao Te Ching, 16
Taoism, 15–17, 16, 18, 27
Temple of Heaven, Peking, 16, 22
tengus, 111
theatre see drama
themes, 8–10, 52
Theravada Buddhism, 59
Tian, 39
Tiandi, 35–6
Tianlong, 24
Tibet, 69
Tofukugi temple, 119
Tokoro, 102
Tokuwan:
Fukei, 102
tomb figures, 35, 92
tomb guardians, 23, 28
transmigration of souls, 17–18
Treta Yuga, 58
Trinavarta, 74
Tripitaka see Xuang Zang
Tukiyomi, 110

U

the underworld, 18,

24, 44–5, 44
Utamaro

V

Vaikuntha, 54
vajra, 56
Vassantara Jataka tale, 81
Vasudev, 72–3
Vasuki, 64
Vayu, 77
Vedic religion, 52, 56
Vega, 31
Vessantara, 81
viharas, 8
vinas, 60, 62
Vishnu, 51, 52–3, 54, 56, 60, 61, 64, 67, 70–2, 70–2, 76
Vishnu Samabranahama, 70
Vritra, 56

W

waka poetry, 102
The Warring States, 15
water, 38
Waves at Matsushima (Sotatsu), 99
weapons, 14
Wenchang, 24
wind god see Vayu
world pictures, 8–9, 24, 26, 57, 58, 60
Wo-usu, 95

X

Xi you ji (Wu Cheng'en), 43, 43
Xihe, 27
Xiwangmu, 25, 29, 34, 45, 45
Xuan Zang, 43, 43, 47
Xuan Zong, 34

Y

yakshis, 7
Yakushi-nyorai, 105
Yakushiji temple, 105
Yama, 45
Yamato-pime, 98
Yamato-takeru, 95–9, 97, 102–3, 105, 123
Yamuna River, 72–3
yang, 20, 21, 36
Yangtse River, 34
Yao, 28, 35
Yasodha, 72–4
Yasodhara, 79
Yellow River, 14, 34
Yen Wang, 18
Yi, 27–9, 31
yin, 20, 21, 36
Yomi, 106–7
Yu see Great Yu
Yugas, 58

Z

Zen Buddhism, 59, 116, 116, 119–20, 120, 123
zhou bei school, 24
Zhurong, 24, 36

Acknowledgements

The author and publishers would like to thank Ravi Kumar and Crown Publishers, Inc., New York, for permission to reproduce the image on p 55, from *The Jain Cosmology*, copyright 1981 by Ravi Kumar.

a = above; *b* = below; *l* = left; *r* = right

C M Dixon pp 6, 7bl, 9b, 14, 20, 24, 27, 28l, 34, 35, 36, 37, 39, 40l, 42, 43l, 44l, 45, 50, 52, 53, 54, 56, 61, 63, 64, 65, 66, 67, 68, 69, 70, 71,72, 74, 76, 77, 78, 79, 80, 81, 86, 88b, 92r, 115, 116; School of Oriental and African Studies pp 7a, 10b, 11a, 40r, 49, 90, 93a&b, 97, 102, 104b, 107, 110, 118, 121b, 122b; The Hutchinson Library pp 7br, 8b, 17, 18, 23, 29, 34a, 38, 62, 92l, 95b, 104a, 114, 121a; Society for Anglo-Chinese Understanding pp 8a, 9a, 22l, 33r, 48; Japan National Tourist Organization pp 10a, 93, 94, 95a, 98b, 99, 103, 105, 106, 108, 112, 113, 115a, 119, 120, 122a, 123; Reproduced by courtesy of the Trustees of the British Museum pp 11b, 44r, 88b, 98a, 124; Victoria and Albert Museum pp 12, 15, 22r, 26, 73; The Oriental Museum, University of Durham pp 16, 19, 21, 25, 33l, 41, 109; The British Library pp 28r, 46, 59; Chinese Tourist Organization pp 30, 31, 32, 43r, 47; Arts Council of Great Britain p 57; Ronald Sheridan's Photo Library p 58; Michael Freeman pp 60, 88a back jacket; National Museum, New Delhi p 75; Freer Gallery of Art pp 83, 100; Chandigarh Museum pp 85, 87; Kobe City Museum p 111.